Street Crime

Crime and Society Series

Series editor: Hazel Croall

Published titles

Sex Crime (second edition), by Terry Thomas
Burglary, by R.I. Mawby
Armed Robbery, by Roger Matthews
Car Crime, by Claire Corbett
Street Crime, by Simon Hallsworth

Street Crime

Simon Hallsworth

WILLAN
PUBLISHING

Published by

Willan Publishing
Culmcott House
Mill Street, Uffculme
Cullompton, Devon
EX15 3AT, UK
Tel: +44(0)1884 840337
Fax: +44(0)1884 840251
e-mail: info@willanpublishing.co.uk
website: www.willanpublishing.co.uk

Published simultaneously in the USA and Canada by

Willan Publishing
c/o ISBS, 920 NE 58th Ave, Suite 300,
Portland, Oregon 97213-3786, USA
Tel: +001(0)503 287 3093
Fax: +001(0)503 280 8832
e-mail: info@isbs.com
website: www.isbs.com

First published 2005

ISBN 1-84392-028-X (paperback)

British Library Cataloguing-in-Publication Data

A catalogue record for this book is available from the British Library

Typeset by GCS, Leighton Buzzard, Bedfordshire, LU7 1AR
Project managed by Deer Park Productions, Tavistock, Devon
Printed and bound by T.J. International Ltd, Trecerus Industrial Estate, Padstow, Cornwall

To Adam and Lucie

And England still hath bin a fruitfull Land
Of valiant thieues, that durst bid true men stand.

John Taylor, the Water Poet, 1662

Contents

Introduction

It was a cold wet Friday evening somewhere back in the winter of 1988. That was the day I became a victim of a street robbery. I was living at the time in Brixton and the robbery took place along one of the many small backstreets that lead off from Brixton Hill. It happened as I was returning home having visited a local shop where I had purchased a few goods. These I had stored in a small rucksack.

I had almost reached Brixton Hill when I became aware of the presence of a group of young men congregating on the pavement some 50 metres ahead of me. Though, to be fair, the idea of young men congregating together was nothing new – this was, after all, an area with a vibrant street culture – there was, nevertheless, something about the behaviour of this group that caught my attention. It might have been something about the way in which they were observing me, but I think it was more to do with the fact that the road I was walking along was not a place where young men typically congregated.

With alarm bells ringing away, I resolved to avoid the group by turning into a small side street while also quickening my pace. As I turned, however, so did the group. I ran and they ran after me – only, I'm afraid, a lot faster. Unable to escape, I stopped and confronted them. Unfortunately it was not the most propitious of locations – a small lane off the main road in darkness. Things were not looking good. There were six of them aged, I guess, between fifteen and eighteen. Two members of the group were clearly older than the others and these were also the most aggressive and active in what followed. One of them pulled a knife which he held to my throat. He looking unswervingly at my face and emanated what I can only describe as a sense of barely controlled aggression. The other did the talking: 'Empty yo fucking pockets … I said empty yo fucking pockets if you don't want to get hurt.' I complied but had nothing to show because I did not have what they wanted. The talker was not impressed 'Where's yo fucking cash, where's yo wallet … don't fuck with us.'

Despite the presence of the knife and the calculated display of aggression, I felt strangely calm. I knew intuitively that if I said the wrong thing or acted in the wrong way I would get hurt. They were capable of violence. I also sensed, however, that they were not going to hurt me unless I provoked them into doing so. I remonstrated with them that I was a student, I had no money and that all I had was some shopping which I needed. The holes in the pockets of the old trench coat I was wearing provided evidential support for my case. I was not, I was trying to suggest, a suitable target. On the contrary, I tried to suggest, and with some honesty, that I was poor with nothing worth stealing. Convinced I had nothing of value, they eventually left me alone and made off. They also took my rucksack. This was, I felt, taking things too far. The bag after all contained some beer, and one thing I knew with total certainty was that when I finally returned home I would need a strong drink. So I followed them and remonstrated. For some entirely obscure reason they listened. One of the younger men grabbed my bag and left it on the road for me to pick up.

It was only after I returned to my flat that the full impact of what had happened began to hit home. At first I felt an overwhelming sense of joy that nothing had been taken and that what they had taken they had returned. This emotion was, however, quickly replaced by a far stronger one: righteous indignation about what had occurred. The event had shaken me up. It was not fair and I should not have been a victim. I slept badly that night and, truth to tell, my sleeping pattern was severely disturbed for the next few weeks. Dark murderous thoughts entered my mind and I experienced great difficulty in displacing them. My routine activity also changed. I became far more suspicious of all groups of young men. I also kept wondering what I would do should I happen to come across the group that had attacked me.

Did I call the police? I thought about it, but in the end I decided not to. What, I rationalised to myself, was there to report? Anyway, what at the end of the day could or would be done? I hadn't been hurt in any physical sense and nothing had been taken. My putative muggers had even returned to me the goods they had taken. And then just what could I say? I realised early on that I would not recognize my protagonists even if I did happen to see them. Young, black and male – the usual suspects, nothing behind or beyond the stereotype. This was Brixton after all. My attack would not even make the grade of a recorded offence. Like so many others, it would be left to a memory that would fade over time.

It did. I had not been injured and simply got on with my life. But I was lucky. Many other people I knew had been a victim of street crime, and as this book was being written many more people were becoming victims of what the media was representing as an unprecedented increase in this crime category. Muggers, the papers appeared to suggest, were once more on the move and the good society was once again under threat. Ominously, the spectre of the black mugger reappeared and Brixton once again hit the news as the capital's street-crime hot spot.

Following tracks already beaten out by previous Conservative administrations, the Labour government under Tony Blair responded by readying itself for war. The chief of the Law Lords, Justice Woolf, demanded yet more imprisonment for street robbers, most of whom were already being jailed when caught anyway. This was an intervention that slipped seamlessly into the clarion call for 'zero tolerance' routinely made by a tabloid media that had worked itself into a frenzy of moral indignation and rage.

It was against this background, the latest in a long line of moral panics about street robbery, that I found myself commissioned by Government Office for London to study rising street crime in the area where it appeared to be the highest. Ironically, this was in Brixton, my one-time home and the place where my own victimisation had occurred many years before. This book came out of that experience.

Given the prominence of robbery in urban street life and the social attention routinely brought to bear upon it by the media and populist politicians, it came as something of a surprise to find that, as an offence, little had been written about it and the people who were or who had been perpetrating it. Indeed, with the exception of Stuart Hall *et al.*'s seminal work on 'mugging' written in the 1970s, almost nothing had been substantively written about the subject. And even taking into account Hall *et al.*'s work, *Policing the Crisis* was principally written as a critical exercise in documenting the social response to street robbery – not attending to the task of explaining it. This absence of discussion, particularly on the part of more critical traditions in criminology helped frame the principal themes of this book. These will be directed at providing a historical context in which to situate contemporary concerns about street robbery; reviewing how different traditions in criminology have sought to account for the problem; and by developing a framework of analysis I will subsequently apply to explain street crime's contemporary rise in British society.

In the remainder of this introduction I have two aims. First, to define more specifically the objective of this enquiry: what is street crime and how for the purpose of analysis should we define it? Second, to examine how I will approach this objective by describing the structure of the book as well as indicating the broad parameters of my argument.

At first sight, the term 'street crime' appears a relatively obvious and straightforward crime category. One that, taken at face value, should embrace all crimes perpetrated in publicly shared space. And it is true that in some cases this omnibus meaning of the word is indeed deployed by various policy makers – not to say academics. For example, in recent Home Office advice circulated to local crime-reduction partnerships in London, the term street crime is used in ways that include street robbery but which also make reference to gun crime. In a far more systematic attempt to get to grips with the meaning of 'street crime', Les Johnson has produced a comprehensive analysis of the various offences that could be included in the term (Johnson 1998). This omnibus use of the term, however, is not the way it is deployed by the police, who code it in ways that impose a far more prescriptive meaning. As an offence, street crime is used to:

> describe the offences of robbery, attempted robbery and snatch theft from the person irrespective of location. 'Snatch thefts' refer to those incidents where an offender snatches property away from the victim, the force being applied to the property as opposed to the person, and the victim being immediately aware of what has happened (Smith 2003).

What unifies all forms of street robbery is that it occurs in public space and involves the illegal appropriation of the goods or property a victim or group of victims may be carrying. Other offences that may occur on the street, for instance public disorder offences such as assault, are coded in different offence categories and are not labelled as street robbery despite occurring in the context of the street. While this may appear an arbitrary way of coding reality, there is, in effect, a kind of rationale to it. All the offences that fall within the remit of its official police definition of street crime have an exclusive focus on a form of acquisitive crime conducted in a street context. While violence or the threat of violence may well be used, it is worth noting that this may not be the case as, for example, with pickpocketing.

Official definitions, it must be emphasized, do not exhaust the meanings associated with the term street crime. In public and in particular media parlance, street crime is often associated with the term 'mugging', which is not a formal offence category. Nor is it a term routinely deployed by crime-prevention agencies, not least because of the highly racialized context in which it has been traditionally evoked by elements in the mass media.[1] Finally, while 'mugging' might well be the term preferred by the mass media, it should be noted that it is not the term used on the street by young people actively involved in street robbery. In this context, what the police refer to as street crime is most often termed 'jacking'. For the purpose of this analysis, 'street robbery' will be my preferred term. This choice is determined not only because it facilitates analysis, but also because it avoids other unfortunate connotations with which the term is too often associated by using the more generic expression 'street crime', which is far broader and looser.

While individuals may well perpetrate street robbery alone, this offence is often conducted in the context of a group. Roles within the group can also be distinguished, with some engaging directly in the task of robbery itself while other members stand guard as sentinels, ever vigilant for law-enforcement activity. Even in the context of a collective attack, it could also be noted (as I observed from my own experience) that different people may play different roles. One person, for example, may work to distract the victim, while someone else carries out the actual robbery. Weight of numbers may also be used to produce the requisite level of intimidation necessary to persuade victims to give up their material possessions.

While some groups may exhibit multiple skills in the art and craft of street robbery, this is unlikely usually to be the case. Street crime is rather a job in which specialisms are more likely to be the norm. Different groups, in other words, will typically hone their robbery skills within one of the forms identified above. While the media often implicitly identify street robbery as a crime that can only be perpetrated by inherently vicious individuals designed that way by nature, what this image obscures is just how skilled an art successful street crime actually is. To put the message bluntly, to do it well you have to go through a learning process – it is not something that just happens. A pickpocket, for example, to be successful (i.e. undetected) must be able to master the sleight of hand of a conjurer. In the case of more violent street robbers, the ability to demonstrate violence as a competence is an absolute requirement. Knowing where potential victims can be found and identified, and how to avoid law-enforcement agencies are also essential skills. So is the knowledge necessary that will allow for the effective disposal of the goods acquired in and through street robbery. These are, moreover, learnt skills and, as with any skills, there are those who are more proficient than others. The least successful, like poor Oliver Twist, are those most likely to be caught.

Learning requires an apprenticeship, a process by which a nonpractitioner is equipped with skills that will enable them to become an active motivated offender. This in turn requires the existence of a culture where these deviant skills may be successfully transmitted and internalized. As we shall see in our historical survey, these cultures come in various shapes and forms. At its most basic, training can occur through the medium of observation and imitation. In its most developed form, training may well approximate the kind of learning environment you would find available in any legitimate trade – only the qualifications would be notable by their absence.

To explore the phenomenon of street crime, I have divided the book into three sections. In the first I contextualize the problem of street robbery by examining the history of the street robber as he has evolved and developed in British society since the Middle Ages. The underlying rationale informing this derives from the observation that, in our contemporary age of amnesia, it is all too easy to forget the past and lose sight of just how much it informs the present. The second section of the book critically explores the theories that have been proposed to explain the phenomenon of street robbery in recent years. In the third section I develop and apply my own theoretical framework to explain rising street robbery in contemporary society.

There are two chapters in the first part of the book. The first considers the history of the street robber; first in the incarnation of the medieval outlaw, and second as the highwayman of the seventeenth century. As this chapter will show, while we, and often for entirely justified reasons, view the street robber as a folk devil, this has by no means always been the case. Historical study shows that the street robber is a figure upon which a number of far more positive associations could also be projected, as the Robin Hood mythology of the fifteenth century and subsequent stories about the highwaymen of the seventeenth century testify. In the second chapter I consider the development of street robbery in the developing urban context. The chapter examines how the figure of the urban robber changes from age to age. It examines the 'canting' language associated with pickpocket slang, and studies the incredible variety of forms through which street robbery expressed itself in its urban setting. The chapter concludes by examining how, as a distinctly modern capitalist society developed, an array of forces coalesced in ways that would both lead to and produce the street robber as the anonymous folk devil we know today.

The second part considers how street robbery has been studied and, on the basis of a critique of these approaches, an alternative framework of analysis is developed. Chapter 3 begins this process of examination by considering what we know about the street robber, his victim and recent changes in this offence category. As this chapter will establish, unlike most categories of crime, street robbery has risen. Though the rise has been very sharp, it is in metropolitan areas, particularly poor areas, that the rise has been most noticeable. Though older people can be both victims and offenders, the majority of offenders and victims are typically aged between 14 and 19.

In chapters 4 and 5 I examine the various theories – both academic and non-academic – that have been propounded to explain street robbery in the modern age. Though there are many ways of studying these accounts, I opt for a method that involves distinguishing them by reference to the political orientation of those who propound them. My rationale for doing this is simple: the explanations advanced allow themselves to be easily grouped in this way. There are, in other words, a set of common themes that unify the kind of explanations advanced by those associated with the political right, just as much as another set of common themes that unify those who advance their explanations within the political framework of the left.

In chapter 4 I consider explanations proposed by those beholden to a conservative agenda. For commentators who write in this tradition, street robbery is typically explained by reference to what I will define as a deficit model of offending behaviour. According to this model, robbery occurs because there is something defective about the offender or the cultural group into which he or she is born. These defects may arise because the individual is born with aberrant traits that predispose him or her towards crime; or can occur because of problematic socialization processes that are themselves a product of the underclass to which he or she is alleged to belong.

In chapter 5 the views of those who offer a more critical and left-of-centre position on street robbery are examined. Though some important work has certainly been produced, what remains striking is that, as a tradition, the left has been very hesitant about addressing street robbery with the kind of attention it has given to youth subcultures or the crimes of the powerful. When the left has examined street robbery, it has appeared in one of two ways. First, when it has been considered as an issue worth exploring, accounts have typically subsumed its study within wider theories of working class involvement in crime, which typically hinge on various conceptions of class disadvantage and its impact. Second, rather than study why offenders perpetrate street robbery, the onus has been placed on accounting for the social response the street robber generates.

In chapter 6 a framework for rethinking how to explain street robbery is developed. The errors of mono-causal explanations that attempt to define street crime by reference to one dominant factor are identified and the case is made for developing a more complex theoretical model. This is constructed around the epistemological assumption that street crime is a multidimensional problem that requires a multidimensional form of analysis; one in which a number of relevant factors need to be considered both individually and in relation to each other. By revising the routine activities approach developed by Felson and Cohen, a framework for examining street robbery is developed. Street robbery, I contend, can be explained by reference to the interrelation between three factors: (i) the availability and suitability of victims; (ii) the production of motivated offenders; and (iii) deficiencies inherent in the social control response.

In chapters 7, 8 and 9 this revised model is applied to account for the contemporary rise in street crime. Chapter 7 examines the factors that make victims both assessable and available for street robbers to prey upon. It does this by examining changes in the nature of the objects now routinely carried by the wider public. As this enquiry will show, in recent years more people have become more likely to possess the objects coveted by street robbers. This, I will show, has dramatically raised the aggregate pool of potential targets for street robbery. Not only are there more potential targets but the range of desirable goods possessed by potential victims are also relatively *assessable*, often *visible* and are characterized by low rates of *inertia*, all of which increase the ease with which they may be appropriated. This, I will argue, has occurred at the same time that the possibility of access to victims of other categories of crime has actually decreased.

This chapter will also show how target suitability and availability is also shaped by the kind of routine behaviours in which victims engage. Young people, who constitute the majority of street robbery victims, are not only more likely to carry the goods coveted by street robbers, but are also typically located in spatially compressed areas that leave them inherently vulnerable to victimization by motivated offenders they find difficulty in avoiding. Because young people routinely carry goods that can be easily appropriated, older forms of conflict in which young people engage (such as bullying) increasingly take the form of street robbery. This has the result, I will argue, of making it appear that young people are engaging in an alarming new crime wave rather than doing what they have always done in the context of a violent street culture. New patterns of economic development in high-crime areas also create, this chapter will show, the preconditions necessary for rising patterns of street robbery, and do so by attracting suitable victims into areas where suitably motivated offenders are likely to dwell. This factor, I will suggest, can explain why some areas have disproportionately higher levels of street robbery than others.

Chapter 8 examines the forces that act to produce motivated offenders who are both willing and able to perpetrate acts of street crime. Rather than approach the study of offenders in terms which conceive them to be essentially different from the law-abiding citizenry, the chapter argues that the problem of offending is acutely bound up with the ways in which young people have been socialized. At stake here is their successful and ruthless socialization into the consumption norms of the free-market capitalist society. Drawing on the work of Merton, I then indicate how street crime occurs where the conditions for legal consumption avenues are denied. This, I will argue, is specifically a problem for the kind of communities over-represented among the population of offenders. In other words, multiply disadvantaged communities.

The chapter then examines the diverse processes of differential association that may help explain why only some disadvantaged people resolve thwarted consumption by engaging in street robbery. This investigation requires an examination of outlaw culture, the seductions and benefits that can accrue from engaging in it, and the relationship between offending behaviour and the construction of illegal opportunity structures in particular areas.

Chapter 9 considers how deficiencies in existing social control strategy have also worked to create a context in which street crime can flourish. It does this by examining, in turn, five current social control strategies. These include studying the impact of law enforcement; the role of the judicial system; the respective impact of situational and social crime prevention; and managerially driven attempts to improve system performance through integrating and coordinating community safety effect. As this chapter will show, each strategy alone and in conjunction with others failed to confront rising street robbery rates for a variety of reasons.

In the conclusion I develop my own political standpoint with regard to the issues this book has sought to highlight and discuss. Here I develop the case for seeing street robbery not as a problem society confronts and as an outside that must be beaten back, but as a problem of the kind of society in which we live today. A society that engineers dreams of material consumption among a population socialized to believe that this is what the good life must be, while simultaneously excluding vast swathes of it from the possibility of being able to gratify such dreams through legitimate consumption rituals. I conclude by examining the implications of this line of reasoning for how we respond to street robbery before offering some more general advice in relation to the question 'What should be done?'.

Notes

1 The British Crime Survey marks an exception to this rule as it uses the term as a component of the BCS violence typology which it defines as 'a popular rather than a legal term, comprising robbery, attempted robbery, and snatch theft from the person'. See C. Kershaw *et al.* (2000).

Part I
A Short History of Street Robbery

Chapter 1

Outlaws and highwaymen

Faced with incessant media reports attesting to ever-rising levels of street crime, it is easy to imagine that the scale of the problem we face today is so vast that British society has never seen or experienced anything like it before. Or has it? In this and the next chapter my aim will be to situate our current fears and anxieties about street crime within a historical context. This I will accomplish by looking at the historical record, and by so doing study the predecessors of the contemporary 'mugger' as this figure appears in different places at different times; and by considering the social response this archetypal folk devil has generated.

By initiating this historical survey I will aspire to make two different and opposing points. The first will be to reinforce a lesson that has already been made by other commentators, but which deserves reiterating despite the lack of its novelty (see Pearson 1983; Hall *et al.* 1987). This will be to demonstrate that the problem of street robbery is and remains a perennial feature of societies such as ours. It has always been with us and this brief consideration of the historical record will demonstrate just how intrinsic to the life of British society street crime has always been. As this chapter will also make clear, while the robber has always preyed upon victims, the way in which this figure has been represented has changed considerably. If it is a history marked by regularity in one sense, it is on the other a history in which the figure of the robber appears in an array of names and guises. The mugger we feel we know, but how conversant are we with the gonalph, the buzzer, the footpad, rampsmen, the garroter and the nypper?

The second point this chapter will make will be to suggest that while street crime remains a perennial feature of our society, the social response it has generated by no means remains the same. While today we are impelled to hate and look with contempt upon the figure of the robber, this is by no means the way the street robber or indeed street robbery has always been viewed by the public. As we shall observe, while robbery and those who practice it have always commanded the attention of the public, media and politicians, the attention the robber has received has not been unequivocally negative. The robber has, and for a long period of time, also been a figure of respect, veneration and affection as much as he has been a figure of loathing and fear. Finally, we shall see that street crime is a subject onto which can be projected an array of wider social anxieties, particularly with respect to popular fears about law and order, the moral state of society and fears about its imminent demise or breakdown.

While there is a good case to be made for suggesting that people in general, and men in particular, using force to appropriate the goods and belongings of others has a long history, this overview will focus upon the matter as it unfolds in the British context, beginning with medieval society and considering how this offence developed thereafter. By virtue of this arbitrarily drawn time line, the history of the robberies perpetrated by the ancient Britons against themselves and other tribes will not be considered. Nor for that matter will the robberies of the Romans in Britain or indeed, and more recently, the activities of the marauding Vikings who records attest were among the most effective robbing fraternities in history. I will consider the story of street robbery as it makes its appearance in two settings. In this chapter I will consider the figure of the robber as he appears in the form of the medieval outlaw and, later on, the highwayman of the seventeenth century. These, the forerunners of today's muggers, typically plied their trade on the highways and byways that connected village with village and city with city. In the next chapter I will consider the history of street robbery as it unfolds more specifically within a developing urban context.

Outlaws

To understand the figure of the robber as he appears in the medieval world, we must first use our imaginations and reconstruct in our mind's eye the appropriate kind of society. This is a society which was formally ruled by kings who certainly wanted to project power throughout the length and breadth of the land but were nevertheless limited in the sovereignty they could exercise. There are two reasons for this. First of all, a considerable amount of power also resided in the hands of the warrior lords of medieval society, which effectively delimited the power the sovereign could exercise. Second, in a world without a professional law-enforcement system, the reach of the law remained inherently limited and ineffective.

As far as most people were concerned, the law and its enforcement resided in the figure of the medieval lord to whom they owed allegiance and to whom most were bound by feudal ties of vassalage and bondage. In a world characterized by a subsistence agrarian economy, the law began and ended either where the village hamlets stopped or beyond the walls of the then thriving medieval towns. Only in these areas could the law be upheld and, more than that, meaningfully enforced. The power of the sovereign or his medieval lords to aspire to a more unitary state of affairs would not occur for a few hundred years. Unlike the kind of society we live in today, there was no standing army and no national police force. Most people lived locally and travelled little in the course of their lives.

A world where the reach of the law was so delimited also implied a world of places and people who existed outside and beyond the reach of feudal law and its authority structures. This was the world of the outlaw, literally 'out-law'. It is in the world of those who lived an outlaw existence that we may first observe the formation of the folk devil we know today as the street robber. Indeed, it is as an outlaw that the figure of the street robber first makes his appearance on the historical stage and in popular consciousness.

The term 'outlaw', however, was a catch-all label used to classify all of those who lived outside the law. Just as a robber could be adjudged an outlaw, so too could vagrants and beggars, rebels and thieves. While vagrants and beggars could avoid execution, vagrancy also commanded punishments that included the use of the stocks, public floggings and branding (Briggs 1996).

Just as the term outlaw could embrace an array of felonies, so too could it include people from an array of social classes – a fact that would distinguish the street robber of yesterday with those of today who derive from a more uniform socio-economic position in society. The term covered serfs who had managed to escape from the brutality of their lords, those who wandered as beggars, and those who had been forced from their land by others. It could also include unemployed soldiers and various members of the medieval aristocracy.

If we consider the motives that would lead some in the direction of an outlaw existence where the principal means of subsistence would be obtained through robbery, a number of factors need to be considered. Some of these factors help explain a general motive to engage in robbery. Others, however, are more specific to the class of people whose engagement we are trying to explain.

At the most general level, participation in forms of highway robbery were motivated by immediate economic concerns. It was a means by which subsistence could be gained, and engagement in this risky and dangerous livelihood was very much determined by the fact that the person involved either had no space within legitimate medieval society or had been expelled by it. Though, as we have already noted, the punishment for being an outlaw robber was severe, another motive for engaging in robbery was the sheer ineffectiveness of the law and law enforcement. In other words, the possibility of getting away with such crimes was considerable. In a world where the 'King's Peace' was confined only to centres of 'civilization', much of the country remained a lawless unpacified no-go area where people would only venture if well armed and well prepared.

In the case of soldiers, their participation in robbery could be explained in the following terms. Having returned from a war (often in great numbers), they were often unable to find secure employment in a legitimate occupation, and consequently turned to robbery because it offered them the possibility of engaging in a trade they were well equipped to engage in. While most men in medieval society were armed, soldiers were actively trained in the use of arms, which made them inherently more dangerous and consequently more proficient in robbery than others (Kaspersson 2003). In a medieval lament entitled *The Outlaw Song*, this motive is attributed directly to the singer's engagement in robbery:

> I have served my lord the King in peace and war,
> in Flanders, Scotland, in Gascony, his own land;
> but now I do not know how to provide for myself;
> all my time I've wasted in pleasing such a man.
> [. . .]
>
> Whoever began this business
> will never amend in his life.
> I tell you the truth, there is too much sin in it,
> because for fear of prison many will turn robber.
> [. . .]
>
> Some will become robbers who never used to be,
> who dare not lead a peaceful life for fear of jail;
> they lack what it takes to keep them alive each day.
> Whoever began this business embarked on a great task
> (Isabel 1953)

While many robbers were likely to derive from the cast of soldiers who were forced to dwell beyond the highly limited boundaries of medieval society, it was also a practice in which the more privileged ranks of medieval order could engage. While this may well appear surprising, it is worth remembering that the medieval aristocracy were by no means the privileged domesticated class they would subsequently become under the force of what Elias terms the 'civilizing process' (Elias 1978). In the Middle Ages, they were first and foremost a violent warrior class attached to decidedly warrior-like principles. They could and would condone robbery and a multitude of other evils as well. This was a fact recorded with considerable sarcasm by one anonymous Franciscan friar in 1317, who also noted with irony not only their extensive participation in robbery, but that involvement in such acts was obscured through the use of less stigmatizing labels such as 'shaveldour' and 'ryfelour'.

> Take note that among all nations the English may return thanks to God for a special privilege. For it is said that Ireland and Wales are overrun with robbers, who steal their neighbours' cows, oxen and other cattle, on account of which they are openly called 'robbers'. But in England — may God be praised — this is not the case. What do we find instead? Among us, gentlemen are called 'shaveldours' and 'ryfelours'. For men of this kind break into the treasure-houses of the great, carry off property, drive away herds, plunder churchmen, nor does this touch their consciences; instead, they are hugely delighted when they can plunder an abbot, a prior or another monastic, and they say: 'Undoubtedly it was God's will that such a peasant, monk or friar encountered us today.' It seems to them that whatever they do, they do justly and with reason. And so they do nothing for which they do not know how to come up with reasons that appear to be satisfactory, as a result of the lying way they disguise them and misrepresent them. (cited in Spraggs 2001)

Fourteenth-century records identify some of these gentleman robber fraternities by name. Among these are the notorious Folville brothers and their compatriots the Coterals who plied their trade between 1321 and 1326. The Folville brothers were led by one Richard de Folville, rector of Teigh in Rutland, who was, according to the historical record, 'a wild and daring man, and prone to acts of violence' (Spraggs 2001). Having been adjudged by Trailbaston Judges to be outlaws, a fact that evidently disturbed him, Richard retaliated by taking one Richard De Willoughby, a King's Justice, prisoner in 1321. According to Henry of Knighton's *Chronicle*:

He was led into a nearby wood to a company of confederates and there, under compulsion, paid a ransom for his life of ninety marks, after swearing on oath that he would always comply with their instructions. (Bellamy 1964)[1]

By the Tudor period it would appear that little had changed. As Harrison, a commentator of the period, had occasion to note, the gentry were by no means innocent of robbery, though he also draws attention to the fact that it was a livelihood also engaged in by those lower down the social order. In particular, by those who found themselves either without wages or with wages that were too low to support them.

... Certes there is no greater mischeefe doone in England than by robberies, the first by yoong shifting gentlemen, which oftentimes doo beare more port than they are able to mainteine. Secondlie by seruingmen, whose wages cannot suffice so much as to find them breeches; wherefore they are now and then constreined, either to keepe high waies, and breake into the wealthie mens houses with the first sort, or else to walke vp and downe in gentlemens and rich farmers pastures, there to see and view which horses feed best, whereby they manie times get something, although with hard adventure. (Spraggs 2001)

While it would appear that highway robbery was a specifically illegal act recognized as such by most people, the reality was far more complex than this. Armies of this period, including the 'honourable' crusaders of the thirteenth century, were also engaged in the business of robbery and on a vast scale. Indeed it is evident that it was specifically in order to obtain plunder that would provide the second and third sons of the medieval aristocracy with a material incentive to sign up for war in the first place. The same motive also provided a material incentive to the foot soldiers. It is from this practice that the term 'freebooter' derives.

Robbery in medieval society was therefore by no means perpetrated by the class of outlaws alone. If we look at the complex tribal conflicts between lords, each attempting to expand his landholding, or lay claim to that of another on the basis of some dynastic quarrel over succession, robbery appears as an intrinsic aspect of life at this time. Together with violence, in a society that had by no means been pacified, robbery is a trade in which the medieval lords excelled. Given that, there is a good case to be made for suggesting that England's early history was indeed grounded in robbery and violence. Indeed, all that separated the noble from the outlaw was not a greater or lesser capacity to engage in law-abiding behaviour. It was rather the case that, in the brutal and competitive struggle in which the medieval order engaged, some robber bands were better equipped by force of arms to win out against others. This would confer, not least, the power to define what the law was and who the outlaws would be.

How, though, did the public perceive the figure of the outlaw? It is at this point that we must note some distinct differences in the way in which people responded to the dangers of being robbed by outlaws and the way in which the figure of the outlaw was represented in music, folklore and literature. When it came to the reality of dealing with the threat of being robbed, most people took considerable steps to avoid it. For the most part this meant travelling in company, and ideally with arms for the sake of protection. This habit would remain until the eighteenth century, after which time the highways became more secure as society itself became increasingly pacified. William Harisson, a commentator on travel in early sixteenth-century England, describes the extensive preparations that the travelling public had to take:

> ... the honest traveller is now inforced to ride with a case of dags at his sadle bow, or with some pretie short snapper, whereby he may deale with them further off in his owne defense, before he come within the danger of these weapons. Finallie, no man trauelleth by the waie without his sword, or some such weapon, with us except the minister, who commonlie weareth none at all, vnlesse it be a dagger or hanger at his side. (cited in Spraggs 2001)

In various fictional representations, the figure of the outlaw commanded an altogether different and far more positive response. He would become known, in a serious of incarnations that culminate with the romances of Robin Hood, as an altogether more noble character, forced by the evil deeds of others into perpetrating robbery which he engaged in with audacity and courage. As Gillian Spraggs observes:

> The outlaw of legend is depicted as an innocent man, driven by powerful enemies to live outside society. He takes refuge in the forest, where he survives by robbery and poaching. But these crimes are viewed as necessary and justifiable. In time, he finds a chance to revenge himself, and vindicate his essential innocence. Then he returns in triumph to live on the right side of the law. (Spraggs 2001)

While early romances of the eleventh and twelfth centuries celebrated the activities of Robin by stressing his capabilities as a successful robber (a point to which we will have occasion to return later), the Robin Hood of legend was not originally of noble birth. He was rather a product of the yeoman class: a free-born man. It would not be until the fifteenth century that Robin would find himself appropriated by the nobility and, as Hobsbawn observed, it would only appear at this time that his motives for robbery were in order to take from the rich to give to the poor (Hobsbawn 2000). In his early incarnation it was his audacious exploits as a successful robber that commanded far and away the most attention. As Hobsbawn also notes, what the peasantry would identify with in the figure of Robin hood was a hero who, if not committed to the creation of a better world, at least opposed the injustice of this one and in so doing kept alive the flame of hope for those with little.

While we tend to remember Robin and his Merry Men, we have also lost sight of many at one time equally notorious outlaws, widely known and celebrated and from whom the Robin Hood myths would draw much of their material. Such myths, for example, included the Anglo-Norman romance of Fouke le Fitz Waryn, and the Tale of Gamelyn. Offering a later, but fascinating folk insight into the legend of the honourable outlaw, Groce's 1811 dictionary also refers to one 'Jack of Legs', a giant said to be buried in Weston church near Baldock. This man 'says Salmon'

> … as fame goes lived in a wood here, and was a great robber, but a generous one; for he plundered the rich to feed the poor: he generally took bread for this purpose from the Baldock Bakers, who catched him at an advantage, put out his eyes, and afterwards hanged him at a knoll in Baldock field. (Harris 1971)

What these legends do attest – and this is something we shall also see when we consider the figure of the highwayman – is that the robber outlaw or robber *per se* was never considered by the wider public as an unmitigated figure of evil. He was not in other words perceived in quite the way in which we are now enjoined to view the figure of the street mugger today: as an embodiment of evil we are taught to fear and hate. Clearly the outlaw and the robber certainly possessed a folk devil status, but folk devils do not always, as the Robin Hood legends attest, inspire universal hatred. Thus we find in medieval society, not least in the way the figure of the outlaw was evoked in the Elizabethan age, a representation of the outlaw as an ultimately honourable being, and robbery itself as by no means a dishonourable trade. At certain periods it is evident that the robber could symbolize something entirely noble.

Indeed it was an occupation that could on occasions be considered akin to a national trait that could be actively celebrated. It was in this spirit that John Taylor the Water Poet would state in his 1622 prose poem 'An Arrant Thief':

> And England still hath bin a fruitfull Land
> Of valiant Thieues, that durst bid true men stand.
> (Taylor 1973 (1630)).

Others offered a similar refrain, reflecting the mood of a public that was by no means supportive of the forces of law and order or indeed of respectable society. Nor would such a world occur until the nineteenth century, and even then its appeal was still far from universally accepted. Up until that time the robber could be viewed as a heroic figure; an outsider by no means considered an enemy of the people. In fact, as this quote from Thomas Wilson in 1572 suggests, robbery could be used to identify a national trait by no means widely condemned.

> Theaft is counted so horrible amongst some nations, that men commonly will rather sterve then steale, and here in England he that can robbe a man by the hygh waye is called a tall felowe. (Wilson 1925)

As the medieval ages drew to a close, the term 'vagabond' gradually came into being to denote the space once occupied by the outlaw. It remained, however, a catch-all term into which, like the term outlaw, could be projected everyone of whom the Tudors and later the Stuarts would disapprove (Briggs 1996). Robbery on the highway, however, still appeared as a significant crime in Elizabethan society, though its presence was certainly far less pronounced than crimes of theft against property. Between the years 1559 and 1602, of all the felonies recorded in Essex by the assizes, robbery (collated together with burglary and forcible assault) made up 18 per cent of the total number of offences. This contrasts with a figure of 66 per cent for theft from buildings. Witchcraft, for those interested in such things, represented 7 per cent of the total (Briggs 1996).

Just as developments in the means of production would, as Marx would observe, drive medieval society into the age of capitalism, such developments also changed the way in which robbery would henceforth be accomplished. Whereas in medieval society swords and bows would have been the tools principally used to perpetrate robbery, from the Tudor period onwards it was a trade increasingly plied with pistols a fact starkly recognized by the Elizabethan authorities.

… it is a common thing for the thieves to carry pistols whereby they either murder out of hand before they rob, or else put her subjects in such fear that they dare not resist, their lordships are requested to take such steps as may be necessary to redress this mischief (cited in Spraggs 2001)

By the seventeenth century the medieval outlaw existed as no more than a folk hero celebrated in myths, song and literature. And it is in this highly romanticized form that the legend of Robin Hood continues today in its Hollywood incarnation. By the early seventeenth century, robbery still remained an occupational hazard for the travelling public. Indeed, the highways and byways of England were no safer than they had been in the times of the Tudors, even though England was now well on the way to becoming a more pacified society. In 1617, however, a new way of describing the street robber had appeared. Henceforth, and up until the late eighteenth century, this most durable of folk devils would now be known as the highwayman.

The highwayman

As with the medieval outlaw, the highwayman likewise enters history in an ambivalent form; as much a figure of myth and legend as a menace to be shunned and feared by all. Like the outlaw robber, the highwayman would also inspire poems, plays and songs testifying to his (and occasionally her) tenacious exploits. Like the outlaw, highwaymen would also inspire fear on the part of the travelling public on whom they preyed and as with the outlaw, the punishment dealt out to convicted highwaymen was harsh and brutal (Linebough 1991).

What also aligns the medieval outlaw with the seventeenth-century highwayman is that they were both livelihoods that could be practised by the gentry and soldiers as well as by the poor. Highway robbery, in other words, from its medieval beginnings to its eighteenth-century incarnation, was always an occupation that attracted adherents from across the social spectrum. Why this is so remains an interesting question. To an extent it is quite possible that the historical sources are somewhat biased in their accounts. In effect, the literate class was also the affluent class, and were therefore more likely to be fascinated with tales of degenerate or fallen nobility than they were with a class of vagabonds viewed as subhuman to begin with. This would certainly be the predominant view of the robber mediated through the thriving trade in popular crime literature of the time. This genre, or 'cony catching' literature as it was known, was associated closely with figures such as

Decker and Greene who, writing in the seventeenth century, can be considered the founding fathers of crime writing in British social life.

The reality of life among the gentry, however, points to a world in which matters such as a civil war, inheritance laws, debts and extravagance did indeed create the preconditions that could lead certain young men to engage in highway robbery. That said, in comparison with those who were called 'to ride the acomp' from poorer backgrounds, the more affluent of these robbers formed but a minority. Though the tale of the gentleman highwayman would continue through to the end of the eighteenth century, the gentlemanly aspect of the crime would come to be perceived as the way in which the robbery was perpetrated, and not as a reference to the social class of the robber. It is this fact, far more than the class of origin, that has bequeathed to posterity the romantic image of the gentleman highwayman.[2] By the end of the eighteenth century the highwayman would become, like the figure of the outlaw before him, no more than a figure of legend.

From the eighteenth century onwards, street crime would figure predominantly as a pursuit perpetrated principally by poor people who dwelt in predominantly urban settings. Unemployed soldiers figure prominently, as do apprentices who, bored of a life given over to drudgery and poverty, turn to robbery for their livelihoods. In his study of the London hanged, Linebough also noted a significant over-representation of butchers among highwaymen (Linebough 1991). That brief and uniquely democratic moment in British history when both rich and poor would engage in robbery on the king's highway thus came to an end. Before we leave the gentleman highwayman behind, however, it is worth noting just how powerful an impact this figure had on the public's imagination. Indeed, such would be the power and charisma attached to these villains that they came to command the respect not only of the public at large but also, as we shall see, their affluent victims.

While Dick Turpin remains far and away the most famous of the highwaymen of the eighteenth century, his fame was largely derived from the exploits of other memorable highwaymen who preceded him and who engaged in the very acts for which he would subsequently be remembered. This cast list included such figures as Gamaliel Ratsey, Captain James Hind and Claude Du Vall – criminals well known in their day, and whose short and brutal lives we will now consider.

The highwayman did not, of course, suddenly appear out of nowhere, perpetrating new crimes or old crimes in new ways. The term simply marks a change in semantic fashion: an attempt to rethink an old villain in a way that would appeal to the contemporary audience. The term was also only one among many others that were in popular parlance between the sixteenth and the eighteenth centuries, so the highwayman could also appear as a High Toby or a Knight of the Road. What appears to have cemented the term 'highwayman' into our historical consciousness was the fact that it was an expression that became synonymous with the activities of a procession of famous robbers whose notoriety derived both from their exploits and from the way these were subsequently mediated in literary form. In many respects they do fulfil the criteria for the role of the social bandit, even if Hobsbawn remains adamant that the highwayman should not be viewed this way (Hobsbawn 2000). For many, these robbers did perform a nascent political role, which lay precisely in their struggle with the forces of law and in their robbery of the class of exploiters.

While it is difficult to identity any one person responsible for setting in motion the cult of the highwayman, it is with Gamaliel Ratsey, a gentleman soldier of the early seventeenth century, and Captain James Hind that the myths begin to assume the form that would persist for the next 200 years (Spraggs 2001).

Hanged in 1605, having committed a number of notorious robberies, Ratsey's life became the subject of a number of popular stories. These, as Spraggs observes, would come to assume the status of models around which later stories, subsequently attributed to other highwaymen, would coalesce.

In terms of content, there are a number of similarities that unify these robber narratives. All converge on the figure of a man (and very occasionally a women) who is forced to make his living by robbery, often as a consequence of forces beyond his control.[3] Having taken to a life of robbery, however, it is a trade which is then undertaken with honour, decency and, not least, a sense of humour. Though capable of using violence, it is the capacity to avoid using it and indeed a repugnance at using it unnecessarily that renders highwaymen both folk heroes as well as gentlemen. While many of their victims are indeed innocent, it is also the case that some are not and that by virtue of this their victimization is implicitly justified. Like all noble social bandits, they are generous to the poor and chivalrous to women. Within the highwaymen narrative, there is an implicit sense that there is a tragic moral destiny at work that will invariably culminate in the hero being caught before being put violently to death. The law can be avoided (and their notorious capacity to evade capture remains a core feature of the legend) but cannot be circumvented forever. Justice will be done and, importantly, must be seen to be done. Inevitably the hero is caught, found guilty and sentenced to death. The stories conclude with the hero facing execution with equanimity and dignity, well respected and loved by all.

Captain Hind's story exemplifies this narrative. Born the son of a saddler in Chipping Norton in 1618, Hind became apprenticed to a butcher from whose mistreatment he eventually escaped. Having moved to London he subsequently met one Thomas Allen, a 'notorious highwayman', and turned to a career in robbery. When the Civil War began, Hind sided with the Royalists and fought with them at the Battle of Worcester. By the end of the war he had returned to a life of crime and was eventually captured and arraigned before Judge Warberton for killing George Sympson (who had attempted to capture him), whereupon he was found guilty of wilful murder. Having been condemned for high treason, he was hung, drawn and quartered on 24 September 1652 at Worcester. He was thirty-four years old. In his final speech he declared (in mitigation) that his crimes had been perpetrated against Cromwell's Republican Party. The *Newgate Calender* (1779) records that 'nothing troubled him so much as to die before he saw his Royal master established on his throne, from which he was most unjustly and illegally excluded by a rebellious and disloyal crew, who deserved hanging more than him' (*Newgate Calender* 1779). His head was subsequently displayed at Bridge Gate over the River Severn, while the rest of his remains were dispersed to other gates in the city.

If these are the bare facts of his life, it is in the manner in which he is alleged to have committed his robberies that his fame largely rests. That he could be positioned as an enemy of Cromwell and his Puritan followers also played decisively in his favour in the age of the restoration. In this sense he was not only honourable but a patriot as well, a point affirmed by a contemporary poem:

> Our English Hero sought no Crown,
> Nor that more pleasing Bait, Renown;
> But just to keep off Fortune's Frown.
>
> Yet when his Country's Cause invites,
> See him assert a Nation's Rights!
> A Robber for a Monarch fights!
>
>
> If in due Light his Deeds we scan,
> As Nature points us out the Plan,
> Hind was an honourable Man
> (Johnson 1734).

What is interesting about Hind's case is that he was originally of low birth, a fact that would distinguish him, in class terms at least, from the figure of the noble Ratsey (Spraggs 2001). What is gentlemanly about Hind, or rather that which propels him into the select grouping of the gentleman outlaw, is his involvement in a crime category that had been redefined by the media at the time as itself being gentlemanly. It was not something, in other words, he had inherited from birth; it was something he accomplished by robbing in the right way.

While the details of his biography certainly testify to Hind's status as a gentleman, just as important are the audacious robberies he committed. For it is these acts that exemplify the highwayman as a bold, honourable, chivalrous and noble man who must therefore, by extension be a gentleman, because these qualities embody what a gentleman is supposed to be. A contemporary biography describes how Hind allegedly perpetrated his first robbery under the tutelage of Allen. Hind, having intercepted a group of gentlemen on Shooters Hill, bids them:

> … Stand, and deliver such money as they had, otherwise he would presently be their death; The Gentleman not willing to die, presently gave him Ten pounds, which was all the Gentleman had; Hind seeing it was all he had, said, Sir, here is forty shillings for you to bear your Charges; in regard it is my Handsale; the Gentleman answered, I wish you better luck with it than I have; so Hind took his way, and came to the rest of the gang; and Allen praised him for learning his Art so quickly, saying, did you not see, How he rob'd him with a Grace (Fidge 1652, cited in Spraggs 2002)

In most respects the lives of subsequent highwaymen conform to the established stereotypes observable in the way Hind's life was reconstructed in popular fiction. All that appears to change is the character of the exploits themselves. Claude Du Vall, the famous French highwayman, behaved in much the same way as Hind, but appeared, if anything, even more gallant and debonair. His most famous exploit, immortalised by Walter Pope in 1670, centred upon an occasion where he was alleged to have held up a coach containing a nobleman and his lady. Knowing that escape was impossible but not wishing to appear frightened, the lady began to play upon a flageolet. Du Vall took out his own and began to accompany her. Having concluded their duet, Du Vall is then said to have complimented the nobleman on his wife's ability and observed that he suspected she could no doubt dance as well as she played. Having danced with her on the heath, Du Vall escorted her back to the carriage, where he then remarked to the noble that he had failed to pay for his entertainment. In recompense the highwayman stole four hundred pounds.

While the story is perhaps unlikely, what we do know about Du Vall is that when he was eventually caught and tried at Newgate, Charles II made an attempt to ask for a reprieve, but to no avail. Du Vall was executed at Tyburn on 21 June 1670 in front of a sympathetic crowd. He was subsequently buried at St Giles, where his epitaph was alleged to read:

> Here lies Du Vall, Reader, if male thou art,
> Look to thy purse. If female, to thy heart.
> Much havoc has he made of both; for all
> Men he made to stand, and women he made to fall.
>
> (Pope 1670)

While embellishment is certainly the order of the day, it is worth observing that there was more than a grain of truth in certain exploits in which highwaymen engaged. Though, having made this point, the task of actually separating fact from fiction remains inherently difficult, as Dick Turpin's famous ride from London to York indicates. Though credited with this astonishing feat, such a ride was never actually made by Turpin. It was a feat subsequently attributed to him in the highly popular novel *Rookwood* written by Harrison Ainsworth in 1834. It was, however, a feat based on fact – in this case a successful attempt by another well-known highwayman of the seventeenth century, John 'Swift Nick' Nevison, to produce an alibi for a robbery he had committed in Gads Hill in Kent in 1676. Having committed the robbery, Nevison rode his bay horse all the way to York, where he then engaged in conversation with its Lord Mayor. When he was subsequently arrested, Nevison was able to produce the Mayor to support his alibi that he had been in York at the time of the robbery. York was two hundred miles from Gads Hill.

Though heavily mythologized, it is clear that the lives of the highwaymen did not readily accord with the myths attributed to them, even though, as a number of contemporary commentators observed, their behaviour at the point of robbery was often quite courteous. This is a fact attested to by a Swiss traveller of the time:

Highwaymen are generally well mounted; one of them will stop a coach containing six or seven travellers. With one hand he will present a pistol, with the other his hat, asking the unfortunate passengers most politely for their purses or their lives. No one caring to run the risk of being killed or maimed, a share of every traveller's money is thrown into the hat, for were one to make the slightest attempt at self-defence the ruffian would turn bridle and fly, but not before attempting to revenge himself by killing you. If, on the contrary, he receives a reasonable contribution, he retires without doing you any injury. When there are several highwaymen together, they will search you thoroughly and leave nothing. Again, others take only a part of what they find; but all these robbers ill-treat only those who try to defend themselves. I have been told that some highwaymen are quite polite and generous, begging to be excused for being forced to rob, and leaving passengers the wherewithal to continue their journey. (cited in Spraggs 2001)

Though Dick Turpin would, like many highwaymen before him, find his life embroidered with the stuff of legend, at the level of cold hard reality, what we know about his life attests to an existence by no means as dashing and noble as it was subsequently reported. Though presented as a lone debonair highwayman, Turpin in fact came to highway robbery late in life. The majority of his criminal career was spent working in association with a number of other robbers (the Essex Gang), who specialized in attacking farmhouses in the Home Counties and who were by no means averse to using ultra-violence to separate victims from their possessions. It was at a later stage in his life, when working with one 'Captain' Tom King from a cave in Epping Forest, that Turpin began to acquire his reputation as a highway robber. By the time he was captured he had killed two people, while terrifying scores more. As with Hind and Du Vall before him, Turpin's eventual destiny was his execution, which took place at York Racetrack in 1739. True to the myth, he went to his death with courage, a fact recorded in a York newspaper which noted how Turpin 'with undaunted courage looked about him, and after speaking a few words to the topsman, he threw himself off the ladder and expired in about five minutes.'

What we can be fairly sure about is that until the late seventeenth century the threat posed by highway robbery remained considerable. British society at this time was still disorderly in ways that it would not be in the eighteenth century. From the time of the Stuarts through to mid-Georgian England, the reach of the law remained limited as there was no national police agency capable of enforcing it. Such law enforcement as did exist remained corrupt and ineffective and it is perhaps this above all else that provided the space in which the highwayman could thrive, largely free from the threat of detection or apprehension (Linebough 1991). At the same time, more highways were being established, the coach service was in full operation and, in a growing mercantile culture, more people were travelling between rapidly growing urban centres. Victims, in other words, were available to be robbed, and were attractive as victims precisely because more of them than ever before were carrying the goods that highwaymen sought to appropriate. The opportunities for perpetrating highway robbery were thus very obvious and robbers took advantage.

John Evelyn, writing in 1699, commented on just how dangerous highway robbery had become for those who sought to travel around London and its environs. 'This week', he wrote, 'robberies were committed between the many lights that were fixed between London and Kensington on both sides, and while coaches and travellers were passing' (cited in Ackroyd 2001). Certain highways became particularly notorious as places where robbery was especially likely. In fact, what we find in the historical records are clear associations between certain locations and the highwaymen who plied their trade there. The roads around Hounslow Heath in Essex, for example, were noted as especially dangerous, as was the Great North Road. It was in the environs of Hounslow Heath that Twysden, Bishop of Raphoe, was shot and killed while carrying out a robbery; that James Maclaine held up Lord Eglington and accidentally wounded Horace Walpole while attempting to rob him; and it was on this same heath that Du Vall would dance. Turpin was known to have worked the Great North Road, as did John 'Swift Nick' Nevison (1639–84), whose gang met at the Talbot Inn at Newark and robbed travellers between York and Huntingdon.[4]

While shrouded in myth and legend, it is evident that fiction was not completely divorced from a real world in which highway robbery would remain a by no means infrequent occurrence for the unwary traveller. What remains to be explained however was the perpetuation of the myth of the highwayman both in contemporary records and in later accounts as a folk hero rather than a folk devil. What was it about robbery throughout this period that allowed it to be represented in such a positive light? Indeed, in such positive terms that even up to the eighteenth century we find figures such as Mary Wollstonecraft feeling able to commend the behaviour of the English highwayman, not only as honourable, but as indicative of the superiority of the English over the French:

> …robberies are very rare in France, where daily frauds and sly pilfering prove, that the lower class have as little honesty as sincerity. Besides, murder and cruelty almost always show the dastardly ferocity of fear in France; whilst in England, where the

> spirit of liberty has prevailed, it is useful for an highwayman, demanding your money, not only to avoid barbarity, but to behave with humanity, and even complaisance. (Wollstonecraft 1989 (1794))

There are a number of reasons that can be cited to explain this seemingly bizarre love affair with robbers and robbery. Before we consider these reasons, however, it is also important to add a note of caution: while the cult was widely celebrated, not everyone participated in its expression. In the eyes of the law, robbery would typically be met with a death sentence, as the tales of highwaymen in texts such as the *Newgate Calendars* testify. While we have good records attesting to the many positive responses highwaymen provoked in their affluent victims, the reactions of more mundane and less wealthy victims typically pass by unremarked and too often unrecorded. Indeed, as Blok has convincingly argued in his response to Hobsbawn's positive evocation of the social bandit, most highwaymen were a long way from being the friend of the peasants who constituted the majority of their victims (Blok 2001).

If we examine the popularity of the highwayman, a number of facts need to be considered. First of all, highwaymen did not appear from nowhere; their presence marks a continuity with older myths about the outlaw robber. In this sense they simply reiterate older narratives, albeit in a more contemporary form. Why tales of robbery and the exploits of robbers were so popularly received is possibly due to a number of features common to English society as it developed from the eleventh to the eighteenth century. Throughout this period we witness a society characterized by incredibly wide disparities in wealth and income. While the rich enjoyed high standards of living the majority of the population were barely able to survive on a subsistence level. Indeed, as Linebough observes, poverty in the eighteenth century was so acute that contemporary historians have yet to explain adequately how the poor actually survived at all. To survive meant living in the context of a life where the spectre of poverty was always close at hand and where mundane drudgery was the order of the day. While most of the population would have grown up aware that there was such a thing as the King's Peace, it was by no means evident that many trusted those who represented it. The system was and would remain for centuries arbitrary, ineffectual, corrupt and repressive; a brutal instrument through which ruling-class rule was secured and continued. These background factors therefore provide a powerful set of reasons why poorer members of society would find themselves attracted to the figure of the robber and also help explain why this figure could be accorded folk hero status. Who, after all, would have too much sympathy with robbery of the rich and powerful, not least when the economic order they controlled was nakedly exploitative to begin with.

At the same time it is easy to see why the daring exploits of the robber could be celebrated. Their ability to evade the forces of law and order, would commend itself to those whose lives lacked such excitement and who would often have good cause to dislike the forces of law and order to begin with. Perhaps of more significance, particularly for the labouring masses, was the fact that the highwayman embodied an active spirit of resistance to the repressive order that exploited them all. Thus, 'riding the acompt', while certainly a trade, was also attached to a particular politics. In their defiance and in their bravery the highwaymen not only challenged the law but actively demonstrated their contempt for it and for the society it sustained. A vicarious identification, in these circumstances, becomes easy to understand. Why would the majority of people actually have cause to identify with King and Country at all?

The fact that robbery was indeed robbery could also be overlooked or, perhaps more accurately, be denied by reference to the many allegedly positive attributes of the robber. Finally, if the scales of justice still appeared to tilt towards the highwayman and against wider notions of 'justice' and just desserts, the highwayman almost without exception was caught and executed. Their brave exit from life, usually accompanied by (often widely distributed popular media) noble speeches, acted to justify their election to the pantheon of heroes, even if, ostensibly, it marked the triumph of the law over those who chose to transgress it.

Of course, different audiences identified with the highwaymen in different ways and for different reasons. For the bourgeoisie, what was served up was a representation that cloaked the highwayman in romance, and it is in this guise – as a dashing debonair hero – that he is largely remembered. Noye's poem *the Highwayman* (Noyes 1928) perhaps best captures this highly depoliticized representation. For the working class, however, the highwayman represented and embodied the spirit of resistance in the face of harsh repression. And it was to celebrate this spirit that ballads, poems, stories and plays were written. Though by no means the only play that celebrated the highwayman, it would be Gay's eighteenth century classic *The Beggars Opera* that best captures the spirit of the highwayman as hero (Gay 1727 (1983)).[5]

By the late eighteenth century, highway robbery had begun to decline and became increasingly rare. According to Spraggs, the last recorded highway robbery occurred in 1831 (Spraggs 2001). By then the figure of the highwayman had already become a figure of history and the stuff of legend. As the State developed, and the reach of the law extended with the development of a unitary and far more effective law-enforcement system, the opportunities for perpetrating such robberies began to wane and would eventually disappear – though not entirely. While the highways that linked city with city became increasingly secure, the same could not be said for the streets of the ever-growing urban centres.

Notes

1 Translated by Spraggs (2002) from Rawson, J. (ed.) (1889). *Henry of Knighton's Chronicle*. London, HMSO. See also Stones 1957; Bellamy 1964.
2 Note the continuity with the Robin Hood legends, many of which were also devoted to celebrating the honourable way in which his robberies were perpetrated. Just as Robin would eventually become redefined as a gentleman, so too would the highwayman.
3 As Rawlings observes, it is often as a consequence of a woman's intervention that the hero is forced to embark on a life of crime (Rawlings 1999).
4 The history of the Highwayman, http://www.stand-and-deliver.org.uk/ great_north_road.htm, 2002.
5 When Brecht and Weill produced their own classic version of *The Beggar's Opera* in 1928, Gay's original narrative was left virtually unchanged.

Chapter 2

Street robbery in the urban context

The development of urban centres such as London is of crucial significance to the developing history of street crime in British society, precisely because urban living created an ideal setting in which highway robbery could flourish. City life, after all, brought large numbers of people into close proximity with each other, including those with goods worth stealing and those who aspired to separate them from their goods. City life in this respect provided an ideal environment in which motivated offenders would consequently have direct access to suitable and assessable victims. Urban centres also provided venues where knowledge of the craft of street crime could be taught, while also providing a ready marketplace where the goods appropriated could be sold on and distributed to other people. The city landscape, with its winding ways and dim-lit streets, also provided a setting in which street robbery could thrive as an industry. City streets had ideal spaces in which the criminal could hide in wait for a victim, as well as offering the perpetrator an array of inaccessible spaces into which they could escape. The grim urban squalor and rank poverty that defined the living conditions for so many would also provide a fertile environment for street crime in all its forms to flourish.

The development of street crime

To study the development of street crime in its urban setting, however, we must retrace our steps and return to Elizabethan times. For it is from this period that the multitude of offences that come within the rubric of street crime evolve and develop, a process that proceeds hand in hand with the expansion of the late-medieval city and its burgeoning economy. The rapid expansion of London is of profound importance, not least because this created the preconditions in which street crime in all its strange complex permutations could thrive. In his social history of London, Porter describes just how rapidly the capital grew between the fifteenth and nineteenth centuries:

> in 1600 it had housed around 200,000 inhabitants; by the Restoration there were trice that number. In 1700 London's population was around 575,000, about the same as Paris. By 1750 it had hit 675,000, while by 1880 it was 900,000, a third as large again as Paris, and London was the world's largest city. (Porter 1994)

As we move from the medieval period into the times of the Tudors, the figure of the street criminal changes in terms of the way in which he is now evoked. From a designation as 'outlaw' it now reappears in its most general form as 'vagabond', an umbrella term used to classify all of those 'idle and suspect persons living suspiciously', as an Act of 1495 described them (Briggs 1996). As with the term 'outlaw', into this same category could be placed all those who offended or were thought to offend the sensibilities of the English social order. The term 'criminal' did not appear until the nineteenth century. The term 'vagabond' performed instead the role the term 'criminal' would subsequently take.

Included within the class of vagabond were those unfortunate enough to be poor and unemployed, and who as a consequence were forced to beg for their living, as well as a class of more or less professional criminals. While both groups belonged to the lowest socio-economic groups in society, what also unified both despite their differences was that whether they participated in crime or not, they were generally, as Briggs *et al.* note, likely to be considered as part of the criminal class of 'rogues'. It would not be until the nineteenth century that more systematic attempts would be made to distinguish between what would be conceived as the deserving and undeserving poor, between those who were criminally inclined and those who were not.

The underworld

What we can observe from the Tudor period onwards is the beginning of a process of development that would culminate in the idea of criminal underworld. This may be regarded as a subterranean economy which, like the formal economy, came complete with its own distinctive division of labour. Like the formal economy, the underworld was also character-ized by an array of different trades. Finally, just as trades in the formal economy develop their own specialist language, this process can also be observed in what would become the growing criminal underworld of urban centres such as London.

Though elite representations of crime would systematically overstate the degree to which the underworld was organized, by the seventeenth century there clearly existed in London a distinct and professional criminal class for whom street crime was a way of life.

The language and practice of street robbery

At the top of the criminal ladder were those who had mastered special skills that enabled them to perpetrate specific street crimes. This category would include horse thieves (the priggers of prancers), card-sharps, and burglars of one form or another, otherwise known as 'hookers' or 'anglers'. The 'angler' was someone whose livelihood was derived by using poles (or 'filches'[1]) to which hooks were attached to thieve goods from shops and houses. The pickpocket also appeared first as a 'cutpurse' or nypper. The term was derived from the fact that purses (or bynges as they were known) were carried at the girdle in Elizabethan England, and to be apprehended required being 'nypped' or cut. To 'nypp a bynge' meant literally to cut a purse. While this practice has roots that no doubt stretch back into antiquity, the first record we have of it being perpetrated in a systematic way dates from the Elizabethan period. As it was during the Tudor era that pockets in garments were first introduced, it is within this period that the pickpocket also first appears.

In his 1811 *Dictionary*, Groce identifies the genesis of the term 'nypper' with an alehouse keeper called Wotton who 'in the year 1585 allegedly kept an academy for the education and perfection of cut-purses near Billingsgate in London'. Groce cites the testimony of one Maitland from Stow, who provides the following fascinating account of this particular den of thieves. Having fallen on what could be termed hard times, Wotton:

> ... reared up a new trade in life, and in the said house he procured all the cut-purses about the city, to repair to his house: there was a school house set up to learn young boys to cut purses: two devices were hung up; one was a pocket and the other was a purse; the pocket had in it certain counters, and was hung about with hawks bells, and over the top did hang a little sacring bell. The purse had silver in it; and he that could take out a counter, without noise of any of the bells was adjudged a judicial nypper: according to the terms of their art, a foyster was a pick-pocket; a nypper was a pick-pocket or cut-purse. (Harris 1971)

While young cutpurses would no doubt have appeared low down in the hierarchy of crime, by virtue of the skills they possessed, they did, specifically if reared to the art from an early age, belong to the professional fraternity of criminals. Below this category and comprising the lowest orders in the fraternity of vagabonds came the beggars. Finally, reflecting the low status of women in society more generally, there were the prostitutes. Together, as Briggs *et al.* note, the beggars and the prostitutes constituted the peasantry of crime (Briggs 1996).

The development of cities provided an ideal environment in which street robbery in its various forms could take root and thrive. Just as fashions in clothing would change, so too would the descriptive labels applied by the public and by the street criminals themselves to describe the art of robbery. While the semantics changed, however, the grammar remained consistent. Street crime was, as it remains today, a fact of urban existence; a perennial feature of urban life and living in deeply inequitable societies.

By the eighteenth century the term 'nypper' had largely disappeared and given way to an array of new descriptive terms, including 'gonalph' and 'buzzer' (Ackroyd 2001). The 'footpad', also known as 'the gentleman of the pad', came by the nineteenth century to designate the street mugger of the Georgian and later Victorian period. They typically operated from spaces within urban centres, with their target the unwary or undefended traveller.

But even these terms, unanchored in legal discourse, are free-floating and at times become interchangeable. In the eighteenth century, a footpad was also known as a Low Toby, while the highwayman became, by logical extension, the High Toby. What compounds matters further is that the terms that were used were themselves products of the class of thieves who had evolved their own rich and deeply textured vocabulary to describe their world.

This language, known as 'flash' or 'flash lingo', was fortunately (for us and for posterity) collated with loving care and attention by Captain Groce (with, it is claimed, subsequent additions by 'Hellfire Dick') and reproduced in his inestimable *1811 Dictionary of the Vulgar Tongue* (Harris 1971). Otherwise known as a 'Dictionary of Buckish Slang, University Wit and Pickpocket Eloquence', this wonderful text defines the various terms by which the criminal underworld depicted themselves to themselves. It also provides detailed descriptions of the different forms of street crime and the manner in which they were perpetrated.

Thus, we find that by the eighteenth century a pickpocket could also be known as a 'File', 'File Cloy', a 'Foyst' or 'Fork', while the expert of the breed could also be termed a 'Rum Diver'. A pickpocket who specialized in stealing handkerchiefs could be known as a 'Wiper Drawer', while a street robber who made a living by stealing the cloaks from passers-by, was known as a 'Cloak Twitcher'. It was as 'wiper drawers' that Fagin's youthful gang of pickpockets thrived, while 'diving' was the craft they practised. Not only could the pickpocket be named in relation to what they stole, but there were also terms used to describe those unfortunate enough to have been caught. In what could only be considered a wonderful expression of gallows humour, thieves who had been caught and punished by being half-drowned (a common punishment) could be termed 'Dunkerers' or by extension 'Anabaptists'.

A highwayman might be termed a 'Land Pirate', 'Toby', 'Toby Man', 'High Toby or 'Scamp'. 'To go out upon the pad' meant to look for victims to rob, while robbery in its street form could also be known as the 'Highway Service'. As footpads typically used their feet rather than horses, they were referred to as 'Low Tobys', or the 'gentlemen of the pad' where they were involved in the art of the 'recruiting service' (highway robbery). As the preferred method of robbing victims was often accompanied by the threat or application of force, the robber could also be known as a 'rampsman', a term derived from the word rampage.

The term 'mugger' is typically attributed to America, where it was an expression used both by criminals and law-enforcement agencies to designate a type of street robbery that included the threat or use of force. In effect, the term came to mean what the English had once referred to as 'ramping'. According to Hall et al., (1987) the history of mugging in Britain only really began in the 1970s when the term was imported from America, where it was used by the police and media to describe what was then presented as a new kind of crime (Hall et al. 1987). It is more likely, however, that the term was a late nineteenth-century English invention which was subsequently exported to the US, where it evidently took hold and flourished while disappearing from its place of origin. In a little-known novel entitled A Child of the Jago written by Arthur Morrison in 1896, its hero, a young thief called Dicky Perrott, picks his first gold pocket watch at the tender age of nine. He brings the watch back with pride to his parents who then beat him and sell it. In what we would subsequently consider a classic technique in neutralization, Dicky remonstrates with his mother: 'It's the mugs what got took, and quoddin ain't so bad … S'pose father'll be smugged some day, eh Mother?' (Morrison 1894) This evidence is not perhaps quite as compelling as we might like, but the idea of street robbery (quoddin) as an act perpetrated against 'mugs' who are 'smugged' does suggest that the term mugger has decidedly English roots. That there was also a play entitled The Mug produced locally in Bethnal Green close to the Jago in the 1870s, also adds weight to this interpretation. The tale of mugger's re-importation however is something that will not concern us here.

Just as more legal and legitimate professions develop their own technical language to describe their activities, the same can also be observed to happen with regard to the criminal underworld. Crime, after all, is by no means something that can be perpetrated without recourse to the right skills, and to perpetrate successfully entailed some under-standing of the various techniques through which crimes could be committed. At the same time, in a world where punishments were severe, being able to communicate without allowing others to understand what was being described was also an important con-sideration. Last and by no means least, in the language of street crime we can also observe a semantic creativity astonishing in the level of wit and humour it was able to attain.[2] To 'fib the cove's quarron in the rumpad for the lour in his bung' meant literally to beat a victim in the highway for the money in his purse, while 'the cull has rum rigging, let's ding him and mill him and pike' meant that the fellow has good clothes, let's knock him down, rob him and flee. To rob someone would be 'to do them over', an expression that remains with us today, while to 'frisk the dummee of his sceens' meant to take the banknotes out of his wallet.

Just as the canting language defined the art of robbery, so too would it designate its variations. A 'flying porter', for example, was a robber who specialized in a racket that involved making victims believe that in return for money he could remonstrate with the robbers (whom of course he would claim to know) and return their stolen property. Needless to say, such an eventuality would not occur, as he would simply take the money and run. This, by the way, is precisely what happened when the intrepid (albeit rather idiotic) investigative reporter Donal Macintyre attempted to have himself 'mugged' in Brixton in 2002. Having successfully managed (after three days of trying!) to have his phone stolen he was approached by someone who claimed to know where the robbers lived and who, in return for money, would retrieve his stolen goods. Though money was exchanged (twice!), this did not happen. The crime was by no means new, the art of the 'flying porter' having a long history.

Street robbery was also an art that could be perpetrated in different ways, and different people would specialize in the art of targeting different victims. To 'fork' someone, for example, would involve a pickpocket thrusting his fingers 'strait, stiff open and very quick, into the pocket and so closing them hook what can be held between them'. 'To go out on the drag' meant following a cart or wagon with the intention of robbing it, while the 'drag lay' involved waiting in the streets in order to wait and rob someone. Unsurprisingly, the 'kid lay' involved robbing young people or apprentices, while a 'bug hunter' was someone who preyed upon drunks.

Given the importance of snow to the lives of Eskimos, it is unsurprising that they have developed a far more elaborate and extended array of terms to describe it than can be found in the language of other peoples. For the same reason, when we consider the criminal underworld, what we can also observe is a highly developed vocabulary in respect of the various forms of punishment on offer. We also find, unsurprisingly perhaps, a similar level of semantic creativity at work to describe the apparatus of the law delegated with the task of administering it. Growing up in the shadow of the gallows clearly fuelled the development of a vast array of terms to describe it. Thus it could be referred to as 'the old evergreen', the 'triple tree', the 'Norway Neckcloth', the 'topping cheat', 'Jack Ketch' (named after a notorious hangman) or the 'drop'; while 'to be stretched' meant to be hanged. The pillory, also a regular punishment, was referred to as 'the stoop', while 'babies in the wood' referred to those who had been placed in the stocks. Even the final journey to the gallows had its own description as in 'to ride backwards up Holborn Hill' which meant to go to the gallows at Newgate. Finally, to prove that some things just never change, policemen were referred to as 'pigs'.

The social response to street crime

If, in the medieval period, the space of the outlaw had been confined to areas beyond the city walls, it is clear that by the seventeenth century the outlaw and the outlaw zone had migrated into the ever-expanding city, which would itself have the ability to inspire fear and anxiety in its inhabitants. Though evidence suggests that the Tudors and Stuarts were well aware of the problems posed by street crime in the developing metropolis, there was by no means the sense of fear attached to it that would begin to surface in the seventeenth century and continue to develop into the nineteenth. For the Tudors and the Stuarts, street crime was recognized as a real problem but it was to all intents and purposes largely contained and peripheral to their consciousness. Though life was dangerous and men travelled armed, there was no sense then of the city of vice that we see emerge by the nineteenth century.

The idea of an organized criminal underworld did however clearly fascinate the reading public, as the rise of the cony-catching literature popularized by the likes of Decker and Greene indicates. And it is from this period, about the sixteenth century onwards, that the myths of a criminal underworld, or, in the language of the vernacular, the 'canting crew', begin to proliferate. At the heart of these representations are images of a criminal underworld populated not only by a cadre of professionals but by professionals who organize themselves in ways that parallel the vertical structure we can observe in more legitimate organizations. Thus at the top of the canting crew is the 'uprightman' (or Dimber Dambler) who, in effect, runs the rackets and who receives the best of the booty and free access to the women who are then mutually shared by the rest of his gang. Below him, the chain of command moves down through various subordinate criminal trades to terminate with prostitutes and beggars.

While there is little doubt that a criminal underworld of a kind existed in places like London, there is little evidence to show that its organization ever matched its fictional representation. The myths of canting that abounded from Tudor times (and which, in different ways, have persisted to the present day) reflect dominant class ideas about criminal organization – not its reality (Shore 1999). By crediting criminal activity with a high degree of organization, commentators were, in effect, projecting their own interpretations onto a field that was far more disorganized and fragmented than they wanted to recognize (Davis 1980). By equating the problem of street crime with a skilled, motivated fraternity who chose a criminal career, so it became easy to lose sight of the terrible social conditions that drove most to participate in crime. It also sanctioned a vision of crime as freely chosen by free agents who would consequently deserve the harsh punishments meted out to those who made the wrong choices.

By the seventeenth century fears and worries about how crime was organized became attached to broader concerns about the kind of places in which crime and criminals appeared. Some areas in London and indeed specific streets have always had a reputation as places it would be unwise to visit for fear of becoming a victim of street crime. Areas such as Southwark and the dockland area of Ratcliffe were always notorious as criminal havens, as were the neighbourhood of Chick Lane and Field Lane in Clerkenwell (Ackroyd 2001). These zones became the no-go areas of the expanding metropolis. Places the law abiding would avoid at all costs and where law enforcement was noticeable only by its absence. By the age of Mayhew these areas had expanded to include Whitechapel and the slum area of Saint Giles. These and other impoverished areas would become known by the Victorian period as the 'rookeries' of outcast London.

Edward Walton, a contemporary commentator, catches well the fear that such areas induced in the minds of the bourgeoisie in his melodramatic description of life in St Giles: 'None else have any business here and if they had they would find it to their interest to get out of it as soon as possible' (Ackroyd 2001). This was a sentiment that would be widely reported by a growing army of urban missionaries who, by the Victorian age, found themselves drawn towards yet repelled by the squalor of life in London's poorest areas.

Just as the highwaymen of the eighteenth century could find themselves projected into folk hero status, we can observe a similar process occurring in the seventeenth century with respect to certain urban criminals who, like the celebrated robber and escapologist Dick Sheppard, captured the imagination of the public. As we move into the nineteenth century, however, the processes that facilitated such identification between the public and the criminal would begin to fade away and eventually disappear entirely. While Mayhew observed in the nineteenth century the customary respect conferred by poor coster-mongers for those who eked out a living through crime, and though Sheppard was considered a hero among the young thieves he interviewed, this was, in many respects, the last audience who were moved in this way (Mayhew 1861 (1985)).

From about the eighteenth century, the romantic idea of the highway robber immortalized, for example, in John Gay's *The Beggar's Opera*, would disappear (Gay 1727 (1983)). Henceforth, the street robber would be reconsidered in an altogether less positive light. From the folk hero of legend, the street criminal had by the Victorian age become a folk devil who remains with us today. So, from the romanticized hero Macheath of Gay's opera, we move by the 1840s in the direction of Bill Sykes and Fagin in Charles Dickens's novel *Oliver Twist* (Dickens 1837–9 (1994)). From a character the public is invited to identify with, we move instead in the direction of villains represented as so evil that no one could possibly identify with them.[3] England's long and noble history of identifying with its robbers had finally changed.

The making of a folk devil

By the late nineteenth century the street criminal – no longer a figure that could be vicariously identified with as a social bandit – had finally become relegated to the status of a predatory anonymous outsider. When the street criminal was now evoked it was as a folk devil with no personal or humane qualities to distinguish it, known only for the danger it represented. In this, a demonic incarnation, the street criminal was a person to be feared and loathed in equal measure, which, of course, is how we are now still enjoined to perceive them today.

This sea change in public opinion reflects less the fickleness of the public than an array of wider changes in society and in street crime itself.

From a perennial but by no means invariably serious problem in the early seventeenth century, street crime had, by the nineteenth century, come to be perceived as a major social problem. It was a problem, moreover, that was seen to pose serious risks, not only to the travelling public but to society itself, whose normative order was perceived to be under threat.

The rapid unplanned expansion and development of the industrial city did indeed create an ideal environment where social factors that would sustain rising street crime could and did flourish. In a world where there was no safety net to rescue someone from poverty, and where jobs for the poor were by their nature grim and barely paid well enough to support a family, street crime in its various forms prospered as an alternative career option. In areas characterized by limited legitimate opportunity structures, illegitimate criminally based opportunity structures will emerge. In the case of London's East End, for example, the legacy of boys 'doing the business' (Hobbs 1988) is indeed a feature of economic entrepreneurial activity in the area, even if the image of the cockney criminal is heavily overstated in the myths that attest to it. In areas characterized by stark poverty there will also be a ready market for disposing of the goods appropriated through such crime, and this economy in stolen goods would be facilitated by an array of middlemen. These would fence the goods and move them on via pawn shops, second-hand shops and street markets.

In her careful and systematic review of the factors that drove young people into crime in Victorian London, Shore identifies a range of common biographical features and life experiences (Shore 1999). The endemic poverty in which they lived, the chaotic family life that many endured, and the limited employment possibilities available to them all created the preconditions for the development of a vibrant street life in which various forms of delinquency such as thieving, pilfering and fighting would become commonplace. In the context of this street culture, pursuing acts to which risks and dangers were attached was part and parcel of everyday leisure activity. Involvement in certain forms of delinquency (then as today) is something young men did. While such cultures could tolerate crime, when it occurred it typically did so as an episodic event. It rarely marked a fully fledged apprenticeship into a criminal career.

The continued failure of the agencies charged with preventing street crime to apprehend street criminals also contributed to its expansion, as did the fact that London's growing economic prosperity ensured a ready stock of suitable and assessable victims. It is evident that from the eighteenth century street crime was beginning to be recognized as a problem, while by the time of the Victorians it was perceived as a threat to the very survival of society itself.

Though rising street crime was certainly a powerful motive that can help explain the rising public anxiety, this was aided and abetted by a growing and ever-more prevalent sense that there were dark satanic forces at play in modern urban development. This perception was articulated clearly in various evocations of the metropolis as a threatening space in which crime and vice in all their forms would thrive. Fielding, for example, believed that the urban fabric itself was in some ominous respect deeply criminogenic:

> Who so ever indeed considers the cities of London and Westminster, with the late vast Addition of their suburbs, the great Irregularity of their Buildings, the immense number of Lanes, Alleys, Courts, and Bye-places must think that, had they been intended for the very Purpose of Concealment, they could *scarce* have been better contrived. Upon such a View, the whole appears as a vast Wood or Forest, in which a Thief may harbour with as great Security, as Wild Beasts do in the Deserts of Africa or Arabia. (Fielding 1751; Porter 1994)

Not only could the evolving metropolis be considered a jungle in which dark forces could gather and disappear with ease, but also as a space in which the possibility of redemption was subverted by the ease with which evil habits could be so readily disseminated among the 'undeserving' and feckless poor. This was testified to by a growing army of urban missionaries, each of whom found themselves staring into the very abyss of human nature and into the very eyes of the fallen.

> There is a youthful population in the Metropolis devoted to crime, trained to it from infancy, adhering to it from Education and Circumstances, whose connections prevent the possibility of reformation, and whom no Punishment can deter; a race *'sui generis'*, different from the rest of Society, not only in thoughts, habits and manners, but even in appearance. (Miles 1839; Shore 1999)

This is a sentiment also expressed by Thomas Beggs who, writing in 1849, found himself observing a race of people who were in every shape and form made essentially different by virtue of the depraved conditions in which they lived:

> A large part of the population were found to be grovelling in the veriest debasement, yielding obedience only to the animal instincts; brooding in spiritual darkness in a day of gospel light, and much shut off from participation in the blessings of Christian privilege as if they had been the inhabitants of another hemisphere. (Beggs 1849; Shore 1999).

It is a powerful cocktail of images that we are dealing with here. Each articulates with the other and each in conjunction mutually reinforces the idea that street crime is perpetrated by a class of criminals that can no longer be identified with. The authors describe real fears about a crime that certainly remained prevalent in urban life and which consequently posed real risks for the urban traveller. Such fears could and certainly were also mobilized by sensationalist reporting of crime in the popular media. Not only did such reporting typically overemphasize the dangers to the public posed by street robbery, but it also began to create the illusion that robbery was so dangerous a phenomenon that it represented a terminal threat to the wellbeing of all, a point explored by Davis in her examination of the moral panic that surfaced in the 1840s to 1860s in response to a perceived epidemic of 'garrotting' (Davis 1980).

Garrotting itself referred to a mode of attack perpetrated by certain Rampsmen. It involved literally grabbing a victim by the neck. While this form of robbery was already known, it was only by the 1840s that we find a huge public reaction to it, which directly followed sustained media coverage about garrotting across England. As with the media response to mugging today, the coverage was sensational and hysterical in equal measure. In the *Cornhill Magazine* of 1863, an editorial read: 'Once more the streets of London are unsafe by day or by night. The public dread has become almost a panic.' In the ensuing crackdown, those found guilty were either flogged or hanged.[4]

If we return to the world of elite representations of the criminal underclass, much is made of the kind of places the criminal fraternity would frequent. Not only is it to be found in certain areas but in specific buildings and places that in effect become the very spaces where criminal tendencies are produced and reproduced. Thus we find vivid descriptions of the 'flash-houses' where criminals were supposed to gather, or of the boarding houses where the young were supposed to be schooled in crime. Last but not least, we also find lurid descriptions of working-class entertainments viewed as immoral by the sober middle-class urban missionaries appalled at what they saw. Mayhew's description of a visit to a 'penny gaff', a popular form of working-class theatre, brings forcibly home the tenor of such accounts. Having watched with heady disdain the antics of a young dancer, he finds himself appalled by the popular reception accorded to 'a funny gentleman' who clearly offended every moral standard he believed himself to uphold.

> The most obscene thoughts, the most disgusting scenes were coolly described, making a poor child near me wipe away the tears that rolled down her eyes with the enjoyment of the poison. There were three or four of these songs sung in the course of the evening, each one being encored and then changed. One written about Pine–Apple Rock was the great treat of the night, and offered greater scope to the rhyming powers of the author than any of the others. In this not a single chance had been missed; ingenuity had been exerted to its utmost lest an obscene thought should be passed by, and it was absolutely awful to behold the relish with which these young ones jumped to the hideous meaning of the verses. (Mayhew 1985)

What these different narratives work to produce is a representation of the robber as somebody who is essentially different from the normal law-abiding public, and as pathologically dangerous in their difference. What such narratives of essentualizing difference accomplish is an eviction of anything that might once have framed a point of identification between the public and the street robber. Denied all humanity, the robber is positioned simply as a vehicle onto which can be projected public anxiety, fear and hatred, and from whom anything approaching pity is removed.

Changes in social control must also be understood as playing a significant role in transforming the figure of the street robber from folk hero to folk devil. From a repressive system that relied for its deterrent effect upon the maiming and destruction of bodies in public spaces, we move by the nineteenth century towards an order in which punishment would centre on what Foucault would term an 'economy of suspended rights' (Foucault 1977). Where once the gallows at Tyburn performed the exemplary role of protecting the good society from its lawless outside (Spierenburg 1998), this space would soon become home to a new symbol of modernity, the penitentiary. What is important in this change is that by moving punishment 'backstage' and out of sight of a public audience, the many points of contact that would once have facilitated the identification between the robber and his class of origin disappeared. Where the spectacle of the scaffold would once have provided a point where crowds could gather to hear the condemned bear testimony to the inequitable order that would kill him, this was no longer possible in a modern order which actively suppressed not only the possibility of physical contact but also eliminated the literary industries that would actively connect the convict with a wider audience. From a pre-modern order in which the testimonies of the condemned would be widely circulated in the form of the 'Ordinary', a pamphlet which published proceedings from the trials at Newgate (Linebough 1991), we see the gradual development of more censorship concerning the material to be made available.

Cumulatively over time, this politics of distance would act decisively to separate the condemned from their public. At the same time, in an era characterized by the rise of a mass media whose political affiliations reflected dominant and elite representations about crime, so the public at large would only find mediated to them a discourse in which crime and the criminal were reproduced in pathological terms. While the rise of criminology as a discipline might suggest a new way of humanizing the deviant, it is evident that in its earlier biological reductionist forms it simply helped criminalize the criminal further, by suggesting that their difference owed less to the social conditions in which they lived and more to symptoms of atavistic degeneracy that were held to drive the criminal to crime in the first place.

Against a background characterized by real worries about an offence that has a long prehistory, we can see projected on to street crime and the street criminal fears and anxieties that were also attached to series of entirely dubious normative assumptions. What these work to accomplish is to represent the problem of street crime in ways that move it away from its point of experiential origin and reconstruct it as indicative of things greater and more threatening than itself.

At the heart of the emerging constellation of representations are three related representations of street crime and street criminals. The first centres on notions of essentialized difference, the second on conceptions of dangerousness, the third around ideas of pollution. As we have observed in the descriptions of the criminal class, what we are presented with are ideas of people who are by nature, appetite and inclination profoundly different from the normal law-abiding citizen. It is in this sense that they are in Miles's term a *sui generic* species of humanity. The symbols of their otherness are evident in such matters as their biology, their appearance, their dress and, last but not least, by virtue of the fact that they have their own language.

Not only is this an alien species, but it is also at the same time a dangerous class, a class that threatens the law-abiding population not only because it is addicted to a depravity it endlessly reproduces among itself, but because this depravity threatens to exceed its points of origin. If the criminal class is a dark force it is a force that threatens to overreach the dark areas in which it dwells (the rookeries of outcast London) and in so doing erupt into the mainstream of social life which it threatens to destroy. Street robbery in effect is its chosen vehicle for injury. This brings us to its third dimension: the idea that it is a source of pollution and contamination. Like a virus, its contamination can spread, and in its dispersal the body of society as a whole may find itself terminally harmed.

By the twentieth century and thereafter, there would only be one representation available by which to describe the highway robber: that disseminated by dominant elites along with populist journalists writing in the expanding news media. This would be as folk devil and as evil incarnate, a figure familiar to us today but not that much different from the kind of representation that already existed by the end of Victoria's reign. The criminal classes had arrived as much invented as an endemic feature of social life (Shore 2003).

While Hobsbawn is correct in his observation that modern urban society does not create the conditions of existence that could sustain the reality of the social bandit, what is interesting is that it continues to sustain its myth (Hobsbawn 2000). Not only in the contrived world of Hollywood with its perpetual reconstruction and appropriation of the Robin Hood myth, but perhaps more authentically in the work of those who, like Brecht and Weill, were more attuned to perceive the political force of the robber in deeply divided and inequitable societies.

Notes

1 Which, etymologically, is where the term 'filching', as in the verb 'to steal', derives.
2 Which well justifies Max Harris's observation that in relation to the 'feeble colourless dry products' of the aristocracy, the language of the criminal underworld was indeed a 'miracle of quick witted creative invention'. See Harris 1971.
3 Though, that said, Dickens painted an entirely sympathetic picture of the Artful Dodger, indicating the appeal of the older outlaw narratives had by no means disappeared entirely.
4 For an examination of other Victorian moral panics around street crime, see Pearson, G. (1983). *Hooligan: a History of Respectable Fears*. London: Routledge. For a consideration of an eighteenth-century predecessor in Chelsmford, see

King, P. (1987). 'Newspaper reporting, prosecution practice and perceptions of urban crime: the Colchester crime wave of 1765,' *Continuity and change* 2: pp. 423–54.

Part 2
Accounting for Street Crime

Chapter 3

Interpreting the data

Before we consider street robbery theoretically, we need to understand the phenomena under investigation. We need to know, in other words, the 'facts' of the matter in order to know what it is we are attempting to explain. This may profitably be considered in relation to what the statistical evidence about street crime reveals, and this will constitute the aim of this chapter.

What an analysis of the available data also allows us to do is to place street crime more firmly in its context. In a media-dominated world where hard facts about street crime are too often lost or obscured in an all -too-successful attempt to sensationalize the offence, what a more sober appraisal of the evidence can accomplish is the task of showing just how extensive and pervasive street crime is.

Before we consider what the evidence shows, however, it is important to draw attention to the limits and limitations that are inherent in using such material. Methodologically it is inadvisable to proceed with any investigation of empirical 'facts' without noting a number of issues pertaining to the way in which they are constructed and recorded. No single research tool is infallible and we consequently need to be aware of what we can justifiably claim on the basis of the research methods selected, as well as the terms we use to describe often-complex events such as those embraced by the label street crime.

First of all, it is important to remember that the term street crime is itself a reification. It does not, as we have already noted, classify any single crime perpetrated on the streets, nor does it signify all crimes committed in a street context. It rather refers selectively to a few, namely those that involve separating victims from their goods or their money in one of three specific ways. These refer to direct robbery where violence is threatened, to snatch, and to pickpocketing. Though most media attention typically focuses on the former – the category that constitutes what the public and media like to term 'mugging' and street youth 'jacking' – it is worth noting that this may in fact form only a small part of the overall street crime picture.

Crimes appear on police statistics if they have been reported and recorded. The problem, though, is that not all street crimes are reported, and it is by no means evident that on all occasions the way they are reported represents the correct offence category. The offences that do get reported may also have intrinsic to them a certain set of biases that can obscure the reality they will, as statistical evidence, be used to represent. If the goods stolen in an act of robbery are relatively inexpensive, a victim may well choose not to report them missing. If the victim is young and lives in close proximity to the perpetrators, who are likely to be older, they may be afraid to report their victimization. If for some reason you distrust the forces of law and order, and this could be the case among some sections of the black population (Bowling 2002), you may not report your victimization anyway. Where, for example, someone is victimized either through having their pockets picked or their bags snatched, research indicates that there is a tendency on the part of victims to assume that their assailant is black, even though they may not have the visual evidence to support that assumption. Momentary encounters, in other words, do not provide the visual evidence needed to make an accurate ethnic distinction. Finally, not all street crime offences that are reported may be accurate. There may well be a number that are bogus in so far as they involve callers who claim to have had goods such as mobile phones stolen when they have not. By reporting the event, however, a crime number is given and a crime event is constructed. This can then be used for the purposes of an insurance claim. What subsequently appears in the police statistics, as a reported street crime, may thus be nothing of the sort. What we have instead is an exercise in insurance fraud.

Given the limits and limitations of police statistics, victim surveys are now regularly used to establish a more accurate picture of crime. Using structured questionnaires which respondents either self-complete or complete with the aid of an interviewer, these surveys seek to establish the reality of crime by directly engaging with a randomly selected sample of the population. The scope of victim surveys may change to reflect policy preferences, but in general what such surveys provide a direct and unmediated access into individual perceptions and experiences of crime and its social and material impact.

In the UK the most important of these victim surveys is the British Crime Survey, which is now conducted on a bi-annual basis. Designed to estimate the extent of victimization in the previous year among the population of England and Wales, the survey was conducted on a randomly selected population. In the case of the 2000 survey, 20,000 households were selected and an individual randomly selected from each household was then interviewed. In selecting the sample population, care was taken to ensure that it was representative of the population as a whole. In this sense, care was taken to ensure that issues around ethnicity, gender, geographical area and forms of housing tenure were taken into account. From the responses given, an aggregate representation of crime patterns in British society was then grossed up by generalizing the findings of the survey to the population as a whole.

Though this survey provides a better insight into crime patterns than police statistics – which is why the findings from the last survey will be considered below – it also worth noting that even this research tool has its limitations. Not everyone selected in the sampling frame may respond, and the responses they give may not in all cases be accurate. As with police statistics, what is included is what people choose to report. In the case of issues such as domestic violence or fights that are not deemed by respondents to be particularly 'criminal', these may not always be recorded. One consequence of problems such as this is that the BCS may well underestimate the true level of crime. In relation to street crime, this is a real problem. Not least is that the survey only addresses a population that is over 16. As many victims of street robbery are likely to be under this age, this is a real drawback with potentially serious implications.[1]

Despite these limitations, the British Crime Survey and other reports produced, for example, by the Home Office and the Youth Justice Board, provide sources of very useful information. They provide an important set of tools that can enable us to identify many aspects of the street crime problem that any explanation worthy of its name must be able to account for. With this in mind, in what follows I will consider what such surveys have to tell us about contemporary street robbery. To accomplish this I will examine in turn:

- Contemporary trends in street robbery.
- The extent of street robbery relative to other offences.
- The profile of the offending population.
- The profile of the victim population.
- The geographical distribution of street crime.

Street robbery in a comparative context

In the context of a society which, in the space of the last two years, has found itself engaged in the throes of a moral panic about rising street crime, one important question that needs to be considered is the evidential basis for this belief. Using data collated from the last four British Crime Surveys, the authors of the 2000 survey examined changing trends in crime between the years 1981 and 2000 (Kershaw 2000). Their findings are presented in Figure 3.1 below, which summarizes changes over time between a number of offence categories.

The table presents what may be regarded as a generally positive picture with regard to crime trends. With two exceptions the level of victimization appears to have decreased over time, and the level of decrease appears to be significant in most cases. The main exception is robbery, which shows a dramatic increase of 14 per cent between 1981 and 2000.

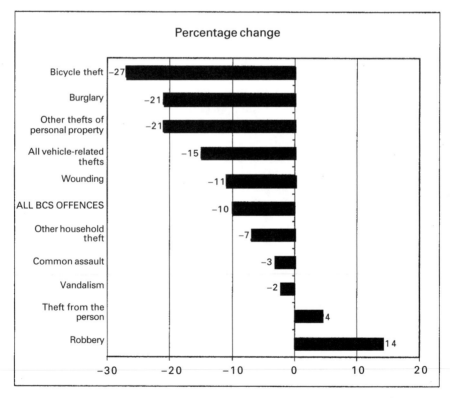

Figure 3.1: Changes in selected offence categories between 1981 and 2000
Source: Kershaw 2000.

According to BCS estimates, in 1999 there were around 406,000 'muggings' in England and Wales. Mugging is defined by the BCS as a composite offence category that includes robbery, attempted robbery, and snatch theft from the person. It is a constituent component of the BCS violence typology. This constitutes, it needs emphasizing, their best estimate. At the highest they estimated a figure of 521,000, and a lowest figure of 240,000 cases per year. As the BCS does not record offences perpetrated against under-16s, even the best-fit figure is likely to underestimate the scale of the problem, as many under-16's are very likely to be included in the victim category. Evidence attesting to this can be seen if the 16-year-old population of respondents are removed from the figures. As the BCS researchers note, a direct consequence of this would be to lower significantly the registered rate of victimization from 7 per cent to 4 per cent. While street crime certainly is a problem that has grown over recent years, what these figures suggest is that it is a problem concentrated among the young, not the old. This is a fact rarely reported by the tabloid media, who have typically presented rising street robbery as a threat to the wellbeing of all.

Though street crime has certainly been rising in recent years, it still represents only a small percentage of the total number of crimes registered by the BCS, as Figure 3.2 indicates.

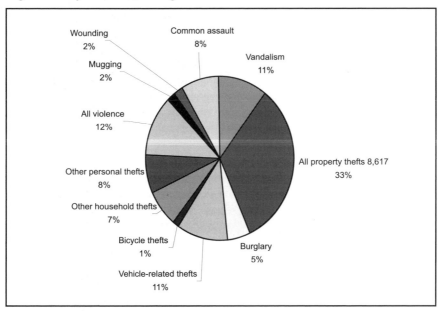

Figure 3.2.   Number of Crimes estimated by the BCS in 1989
Source: BCS.

Burglary, vandalism and vehicle-related thefts all constitute a significantly higher percentage of the total crime figure than mugging, which makes up only 2 per cent of all crimes registered. Indeed, as the diagram above makes clear, street crime remains one of the smallest of the crime categories, even though paradoxically it is among the offences that command most public political and media attention.

Profiling offenders

According to BCS statistics, perpetrators of street crime are typically concentrated among younger age groups. The survey indicated that children of school age committed 7 per cent of muggings, while 56 per cent were aged between 16 and 24 and 33 per cent were older. Below the age of 14 and above the age of 19, the rate of participation in street crime decreases fairly rapidly. Evidence also shows that the age of those who engage as perpetrators of street robbery has changed quite dramatically in recent years. Smith's Home Office study of street robbery showed that the involvement of younger age groups in street robbery has increased significantly as a proportion of the total population of offenders (Smith 2003). Whereas the 11–20 age group made up only 56 per cent of the population of offenders in 1993, by 2000 this figure had risen to 78 per cent. As Smith observes:

> Much of this change can be attributed to the growth of offenders aged 11–15 years, which accounted for 36 per cent of suspects charged in 2000 compared to 15 per cent in 1993. The number of 11–15 year-olds charged with an offence of personal robbery has increased fivefold (by 483%) since 1993. The latest year (2000) witnessed the largest increase in the number of 11–15 year-olds charged with personal robbery. (Smith 2003)

As Smith's study also shows, the growing participation of young people in robbery is not paralleled by the growing involvement of young people in other offence categories such as violence against the person or burglary. As he notes, only 8 per cent of those charged with robbery were aged over 31 years, compared to 32 per cent and 40 per cent respectively for burglary and violence against the person.

Police statistics do not record the socio-economic status either of offenders or of victims. From a detailed factor analysis of aggregate street crime figures collated from different London boroughs in 2002, however, Fitzgerald et al. found that a positive correlation existed between deprivation levels and recorded street crime rates (Fitzgerald et al. 2002). Though the relationship was often uneven, what their work demonstrated was that street crime levels within each borough were likely to account for a far higher proportion of total crime as the level of deprivation increased. The deprivation indicators Fitzgerald *et al.* identified as most significant in explaining and predicting levels of street robbery were the presence of pockets of deprivation evidenced specifically by high levels of unemployment and a concentration of youth poverty. What these results indicate is that class disadvantage is a factor in street robbery.

Though females also perpetrate street robbery, the overwhelming majority of offenders are male. According to the BCS, males committed 91 per cent of street robbery offences, women 7 per cent and both sexes 2 per cent (Kershaw *et al.* 2000). Though predominantly a masculine pursuit, the scale of male offending tends to obscure the steep increase in recent years among young women now engaged in street crime. As Fitzgerald *et al.* note:

> ... the numbers of young women involved appears to have increased at least as much. Females accounted for 5.7 per cent of all descriptions of suspects in recorded cases of street crime in 1998/9 and this London-wide average rose to 6.1 per cent by 2000/01, but masks a range from 4 per cent to over 9 per cent in different boroughs. In more than half of the 32 London boroughs in 2000/01 the rate of increase was actually higher than that for males. (Fitzgerald *et al.* 2002)

According to the BCS, the population of offenders across England and Wales is predominantly white, a finding that reflects the demography of these countries more generally (Kershaw *et al.* 2001). However, the representation of different ethnic groups among the population of offenders changes when different areas are studied. The reason for this is that different areas have different demographic profiles and this fact will be reproduced in the profile of the offending population. In the cases of Lambeth borough and Bristol city centre, Smith found that the population of offenders included significant numbers of those coded as Afro-Caribbean/black (Smith 2003). These areas, however, also had significant representation of black and minority ethnic groups in their residential populations. In the case of more ethnically homogeneous areas such as Blackpool and Preston, however, the population of offenders is almost universally white; a factor that again reflects local demography. As Smith's analysis of police case data indicated, the level of representation between different ethnic groups in street crime did vary considerably. In some cases the rate of representation of a particular ethnic group did appear to reflect local demography. In the case of his sample from Birmingham, Smith found that the representation of Asians among the population of offenders reflected the representation of the Asian community among the population of the city quite closely. In the case of Lambeth however the representation of the black population among the population of offenders appeared significantly disproportional to its representation in the local population even accepting that the area has a large black community.

As Smith makes clear – and this point needs emphasizing – figures pertaining to the differential involvement of different ethnic groups in street robbery does need to be treated with extreme caution. The available street population within an area might not reflect the profile of its residential population, a finding also confirmed in recent surveys of stop and search patterns (see Stenson and Waddington 2004; Hallsworth and MaGuire 2004). It is also worth noting that in the case of police data, not all victims report their victimization and this may well skew the reported and recorded figures. Finally, given that reported rates of street robbery only provide details of the ethnic characteristics of offenders, they cannot reveal anything about the ethnic profile of the offender population because such figures do not take cognizance of repeat offending. It could be the case that a small number of offenders are responsible for a disproportionate number of robbery offences.

While recognizing these health warnings, it would appear to be the case that different ethnic groups do become involved in different crimes, and this cultural factor needs to be taken into consideration when examining the differential involvement of different groups in street crime. Fitzgerald *et al.* found that across the UK, young black males account for a significantly higher proportion of offenders being supervised by Youth Offending Teams (YOTs) for robbery than would be expected given the pattern of their representation in the national population: whereas they constitute 27 per cent of the offending population, they make up only 10 per cent of the national population. In their examination of the involvement of different ethnic groups in different offence categories in a YOT located in London, Fitzgerald *et al.* discovered significant differences in the offences perpetrated by different groups. Nearly a quarter of all white young people supervised by the YOT had been found guilty of motoring offences; and this was true of nearly a third of the young offenders from minority ethnic groups *with the exception of* black people. On the other hand, black young people were more than three times as likely as whites to have been found guilty of robbery, but half as likely to have been convicted of burglary. As Fitzgerald *et al.* observe, what this indicates is that black communities have been disproportionately affected by rising street robbery (Fitzgerald *et al.* 2002).

Profiling victims

If the profile of those engaged as offenders derives from a restricted sector of the population, the same cannot be said of the class of victims, who are drawn from a far wider selection of the resident population. Among the population of victims, however, young people appear over-represented. Just as the population of offenders are predominantly male, so too are the population of victims who comprise 76 per cent according to Smith's research. The specifically masculine aspect of street robbery is also brought home by statistics that indicate that 71 per cent of robberies involve male victims being victimized by male offenders. The precise proportion of males victimized did, Smith found, vary across the different districts he studied.

Just as offenders were disproportionately drawn from lower age groups, this trend was also reflected in the population of victims. Thus, just as most offenders were in the 11–20 age range, 45 per cent of the victim population fell into the same age range. Among the population of victims in 2002, according to Metropolitan Police statistics, 25 per cent were aged between 11 and 15, while those aged between 16 and 22 composed 22 per cent. Unlike the population of offenders, however, the population of victims does include significant numbers of people who fall outside the 11–20 age range, though, as with the offender population, this population tails off in older age groups and among the very young. What this suggests is that there remain significant numbers of very young and very old people who are victims of street crime.

The police data collated by Smith shows that the population of victims has become both younger over time and also greater in number – something it shares with the population of offenders. As Smith notes, this also distinguishes trends in street crime from trends in other offences such as burglary or assault, which remain more static over time when assessed in terms of the profile of their victims. According to Metropolitan Police data, the number of people aged between 11 and 20 who were victims has increased by a factor of three between 1993 and 2002. Among the population of 11–15 year-olds the rate of increase over this period was a staggering figure of 320 per cent, while for the population of 16–20 year-olds the rate of increase was 296 per cent. According to Smith's study, the rate of increase was most dramatic from 1998. In 1993, for example, only 12 per cent of the victim population was aged between 11 and 15. By 2002, it had increased to 22 per cent.

Studies of the ethnic profile of victims indicate that across the UK most victims of street robbery appear to be coded as 'white'. Visible ethnic minorities among the population of victims appear relatively small, though Smith's study did suggest that, as with offenders, the nature of representation varied between areas. Smith's research also suggests that visible ethnic minorities are significantly over-represented in the population of robbery victims. The Metropolitan Police have also witnessed a significant increase in the number of victims of robbery from minority ethnic groups.

The modus operandi of street robbery

According to the BCS 30 per cent of assailants perpetrated street robbery alone, in 41 per cent of cases two offenders were involved, in 11 per cent three were involved, and in 17 per cent more than three assailants were involved. What this suggests is that street crime is overwhelmingly perpetrated by young people operating in small groups. In terms of assessing victim/offender relationships, the BCS findings indicated that 68 per cent of muggings were perpetrated by a stranger. In 13 per cent of cases the offender was slightly known to the victim, while in 19 per cent of cases they were likely to be well known to their victim. Young people were far more likely to know their assailants than older people.

When asked whether they believed the perpetrators of robbery were under the influence of drugs or drink at the time of the offence, respondents overwhelmingly did not believe this to be the case. Only 17 per cent reported the offender to be under the influence of drink and 19 per cent under the influence of illegal drugs. This finding, it could be observed, runs directly contrary to much media reporting, not least the pronouncements of politicians such as the Home Secretary who ascribe drug use as a primary driver of rising street robbery.

Just as the rate of street crime varies across months and years (see above) so too does it vary through the day. By studying crime reports and witness statements, Smith's study of street robbery found that most street crime offences typically occurred at night. Over half (51 per cent) occurred between 6.00pm and 2.00am, while a quarter occurred in the afternoon between 2.00pm and 6.00pm. The rate of street robberies was also much higher at the weekend; 49 per cent occurred during this period.

Different populations, however, were selected for victimization at different times. According to Smith's study, young people were more likely to be victimized during the afternoon, as were old and retired people. Students, the employed or unemployed were more likely to be targeted at night. In the case of the employed, 74 per cent of the sample had been robbed at night, with one-third robbed between 10.00pm and 2.00am. The rate of victimization at night, however, was also contingent upon factors specific to the area concerned. Of specific significance in this respect was the presence or absence of a night-time economy. Where this was present, not only was the rate of victimization higher than in areas where it was not present, but also victimization unsurprisingly rose during the evening period.

Though streets constitute the principal location where street robbery occurs (accounting for 51 per cent in Smith's study), other open spaces such as subways, parks, footpaths, alleyways, footbridges and commons account for a significant 11 per cent of the total. 16 per cent of robberies occur around a range of commercial premises such as banks, pubs, off-licences and building societies, while 12 per cent occur while people use either their own private transport (4 per cent) or public forms of transport (8 per cent).

Street robbery is an offence that can be perpetrated in a number of ways. Different offenders will consequently adopt the method they find most suitable to rob the particular class of victim they aspire to target. In terms of the different approaches, street robbers can adopt an approach that involves a relatively long contact between offender and victim or one where the nature of the interaction is relatively short. Robberies that occur when victims are lulled into a false sense of security prior to being robbed exemplify the former, while forms of snatch where, for example, a bag or phone is literally ripped out of the hands of a victim, exemplify the latter. In his study of the robbery event, Smith identifies five principal approaches, and these are summarized in Table 3.1 below.

A characteristic feature of all the approaches is that they rely upon a high degree of physical activity to perpetrate. If the assailant engages in a snatch, then he must be able both to take the object and escape with it. While the ability to outrun and outwit those who may wish to intercept a street robber is also a required skill, this ability must also be supplemented by the capacity and will either to threaten a victim with violence or use violence as a first resort.

Smith's study indicated significant differences between different groups of victims and the kind of approach adopted to rob them. Males were, he found, more likely to be targeted using confrontation and con techniques, while women were more likely to be targeted using snatch. Both groups were equally likely to be targeted using a blitz technique. Smith's study also indicated that the age of a victim affected how they were typically targeted. Younger age groups, he found, were far more likely to be victims of confrontation and con robberies, while victims of blitz and snatch robberies were typically older (Smith 2003).

Table 3.1. Approaches to Street Robbery

Blitz. Violence is used to overwhelm, stun or control the victim prior to the removal of any property or prior to any demands to hand over property. Violence is the first point of contact between the victim and the suspect. There is no prior verbal exchange between victim and offender, though threats and abuse may follow the initial assault.

Confrontation. A demand for property or possessions is the initial point of contact between the victim and offender, e.g. 'Give me your money and your mobile phone.' This may be followed through with threats and, on occasion with force.

Con. The suspect 'cons' the victim into some form of interaction. This typically takes the form of some spurious conversation, e.g. 'Have you got a light/the time mate?' This is the initial approach to the victim, regardless of how the robbery subsequently develops.

Snatch. Property is grabbed from the victim without prior demand, threats or physical force. This is the initial contact between the victim and the suspect. Physical force is used to snatch property from the victim, which is nearly always on display, e.g. handbag. There is no physical search of the victim by the suspect.

Victim-initiated. The victim initiates contact with the suspect and becomes the victim of a robbery, e.g. a drug deal, procuring sex, etc.

Source: Smith 2003.

The costs of street crime

Crime occasions material, physical and psychological damage to victims. The material costs of street crime can be assessed in terms of the goods taken in the offence. The physical damage occasioned by street robbery pertains to the nature of the injuries sustained as a consequence of an assault. By psychological damage is meant the fear and anxiety that can be induced in victims. In this section we consider these costs.

Though offenders perpetrate street robbery for reasons that cannot simply be reduced to the desire for material goods, this nevertheless remains an important and in many cases decisive motive. In his analysis of the goods stolen through personal robbery, Smith found that money and mobile phones were most regularly taken, though other objects such as debit and credit cards, bags, watches, jewellery and personal documentation could also be removed. Table 3.2 below provides a summary of the percentage of goods removed from his sample.

Table 3.2. Goods stolen in Personal Robberies

Item	No.	%
Cash	986	25
Mobile phone	694	18
Debit, credit, cash cards	337	9
Purse, wallet	327	8
Personal accessories	312	8
Handbag, rucksack, briefcase	241	6
Personal documentation	226	6
Jewellery and watches	224	6
Other	610	15
All property	*3957*	*100*

Source: Smith 2003.

Table 3.3. British Crime Survey estimates of mobile phone thefts (those aged 16 or more)

	1995	1997	1999	2000
Mobile phones stolen*	160,000	270,000	400,000	470,000
% of all thefts	1.1%	2.6%	4.0%	5.5%

*Based on risk figures grossed up to the population of England and Wales aged 16 or more. The risks relate to incidents in which a phone was stolen or an attempt was made.
Source: BSC (cited in Harrington 2001).

As Home Office research confirms, mobile phone theft has seen a steep rise in recent years. From an analysis of the BCS data, the rate of mobile phone theft increased dramatically over the period of the last four sweeps. Whereas in 1995 the estimated figure for mobile phone theft stood at 160,000, or 1.1 per cent of all recorded thefts, by 2000 the figure had risen to 470,000, or 5.5 per cent of the total (Harrington 2001).

Weapons were regularly used in the conduct of many street robberies but were used principally for the purpose of ensuring the compliance of the victim in the robbery act. Actual assaults are relatively rare, and in most cases the weapon is displayed to the victim in order to instil the requisite degree of fear (Smith 2003). Smith's study indicated that weapons were typically used in a third of all robberies (33 per cent) and were particularly evident when a confrontation approach was adopted.

Knives were by far the weapon of choice for most street robbers, and were used in one in five robberies. The use of blunt instruments such as coshes, baseball bats and hammers was relatively rare, and these were used in only 3 per cent of cases. Men were far more likely to be threatened with a weapon than a woman, but women were also far more likely to be a victim of a snatch during which weapons are rarely used.

Though men were more likely to be confronted by robbers bearing weapons, they were far less likely to suffer a physical injury than women (Smith 2003). The reason for this is probably that when presented with a demonstration of overwhelming force (i.e. being shown a knife), men are far more likely to cooperate with their attacker. A snatch is, however, an abrupt and sudden act, and may lead the victim to resist their assailant. Women, Smith found, were far more likely to do so than men. By its nature, a blitz style of approach almost always resulted in some form of injury.

If we compare the injuries sustained by victims of street robbery with injuries sustained by victims of domestic violence, however, an interesting pattern emerges, as was observed in the BCS (Kershaw 2001). Though weapons were far more likely to be used in street robbery than in domestic violence, the rate of injury among those subject to domestic violence was significantly higher. According to the BCS, whereas 70 per cent of victims of domestic violence reported an injury, the figure for what the BCS recorded as 'mugging' was 28 per cent. Though it is a crime in which violence figures prominently, it is not a crime where most victims are injured as recurrently as domestic violence. One lesson that we might bear in mind as we consider these factors is that while street robbery occasions a lot of fear and considerable media attention, its damage is far less pervasive than that occasioned by less sensationalized offences such as domestic violence.

Finally, in relation to the wider social costs accumulated by street crime it is particularly informative to consider these in relation to other crimes in order to put them in context. In a careful and diligent attempt to compare the respective costs of corporate crime and street crime in the US, Winslow estimates that the cost of corporate crime to the economy came to $1–2 trillion per year and estimated that $18 billion were spent each year by the federal government of the US in confronting it. However, the amount dedicated to confronting street robbery in the US was $147 billion (Winslow 2003). Its social consequence is a mass incarceration system that now routinely imprisons over 2 million of the US's poorest citizens, many for street crime offences. As street-level homicide in the US was estimated to cause 15,500 deaths, this may seem appropriate to some. However, it is worth noting that the financial costs of street crime are only 5 per cent of those accumulated by corporate crime (Snider 1993). The number of deaths occasioned by corporate crime was also significantly higher than for street crime.

Among the costs of corporate crimes, Winslow identified workplace injuries and accidents cost ($141.6 billion), deaths from workplace cancer ($274.7 billion), price-fixing monopolies and deceptive advertising $1,116.1 billion), cigarettes and other product injuries (£18.4 billion), environmental costs ($307.8 billion), and defence contracts overcharging ($25.8 billion); and income tax fraud ($2.9 billion). These are yearly costs. In terms of the deaths occasioned by corporate crime, these include 100,000 miners killed by exposure to coal dust, while 267,000 have been disabled. Exposure to carcinogens in the workplace accounts for 150,000 deaths annually.

Despite the fact that, in relative terms, street crime would appear to prove far less hazardous to the public than corporate crime, it is worth noting that (a) it is street robbery that commands more public attention; and (b) when prosecuted it is street robbers who go to jail, not the powerful and lethal sponsors of corporate crime.

Conclusion

What this brief survey of the available data indicates is that street crime is an offence typically concentrated around young urban males, typically those living in poorer socio-economic conditions. Though the over-representation of minority ethnic groups in street robbery is certainly a factor in some areas – notably Lambeth in London – it is not a consistent feature of street robbery across the UK as a whole. Just as young people appear over-represented among the population of offenders, so too do they appear over-represented among the population of victims, though a significant number also come from older age groups.

The data also indicates that while most other offence categories have decreased in recent years, street robbery remains an exception to this general trend in that it has risen, and risen sharply. That said, it comprises a relatively small percentage of the total crime figure. Evidence suggests that cash and mobile phones are the objects most often obtained in street robbery. The dramatic rise in mobile phone theft in recent years is a characteristic feature of the recent surge in street robbery more generally. Though street crime can be perpetrated without the use of violence, violence is a recurrent feature of the offence. Weapons are often used in the perpetration of street robbery and injuries are commonplace, specifically among women, who are also more likely to find themselves a target of a snatch than males. In relation to the crimes of the powerful, street crime occasions far less material and social cost though disproportionate media and political attention.

Having considered as it were the hard facts about street robbery, let us now consider how different commentators have sought to explain precisely why certain groups engage in street robbery, and explain why street robbery appears to have risen in recent years.

Note

1   Indeed it is a drawback with interesting and sinister implications, as Marian Fitzgerald observed (in communication with the author). Given that the government uses the BCS as its privileged source about crime trends, the failure to include young respondents has allowed it to underestimate significantly the real level of street crime, and overstate the success of government initiatives in confronting it.

Chapter 4

The view from the right

There are, potentially, a number of ways in which we can examine the attempts that have been made to explain street robbery. One way would be to consider the issue within different theoretical traditions. Another possibility would be to consider the history of attempts to explain and account for it, while another would involve grouping explanations by reference to the political persuasion of their advocates. Though each of these approaches is potentially plausible, for the purpose of this chapter I will opt for the latter. I do this because there are a number of similarities between explanations posed within right of centre and left of centre accounts that facilitate such analysis.

I will begin this task by examining the explanations that have been proposed to explain street robbery developed by commentators of the political right. The next chapter examines the position of those who operate within a more critical and left of centre framework of analysis.

What unifies the approaches that could be grouped under the banner of the right is that they typically view street robbery as the result of defective individuals born into a culture/community itself considered defective in many ways. This deficiency derives, they argue, from pathological traits identified within the host culture/group/population into which the street robber is born, and this failure is itself attributed to the failure of society to regulate and control the behaviour of the individual and his host culture through appropriate means. What also unifies commentators of the right is that they typically view street robbery as a serious problem that requires urgent attention – a proposition by no means universally accepted (as we shall see) by the left.

Although it is useful to use labels such as a 'right of centre' perspective on street crime, it is worth emphasizing that within this all-encompassing label can be clustered a multitude of different and by no means well-connected or theoretically consistent approaches. Nor – and this also needs emphasizing – are the approaches that fall under this label the product of academics operating within academic establishments. On the contrary, many of the approaches developed within this tradition are non-academic, specifically those produced within the populist traditions of the tabloid media. Though non-scientific, it is still important to consider such approaches, because in their public exposure they also claim truth-value. At the level of popular beliefs about street crime and crime in general, such views also prevail as dominant narratives.

The deficit theory of street robbery

At the heart of right of centre approaches we typically find a representation of the street robber as someone characterized either by an absence of something that normal law-abiding people possess, or by an accretion of traits that law-abiding people do not have. Considered this way, the street robber is someone who is both different and abnormal in one or more respects, and it is this that promotes their engagement in street robbery. If we study this deficit approach in more detail, what emerges is a representation of the street robber as someone whose capacity to engage in street robbery is made possible because of various pathological occurrences that are believed to have happened to them in the course of their lives.

Offering far and away the most reductionist explanation of criminal motivation, there are accounts such as that produced by Herrenstein and Murray predicated on the view that the robber is born into a population that is biologically different from that of the law-abiding, and which contains latent traits that might predispose its members to engage in crime. Much of this debate has raged over issues of imputed intelligence and its relation to crime. The inference typically drawn is that minority ethnic groups/the working class (i.e. the class of origin for most street robbers) are over-represented among the population of robbers precisely because their intelligence quotient is smaller than that found in more affluent classes/ethnic groups. This 'fact' is then used to explain their disproportionate involvement in crime.[1]

Though biological reductionist accounts figure significantly in the work of the right, these are also supplemented by more sociologically based accounts. These typically consider the involvement of individuals in street robbery as a product of their having been born into and raised among a pathological community characterized by a range of cultural deficits that predispose its young towards criminal behaviour. This explanation is at the heart of various versions of the underclass thesis, of which the work of Charles Murray remains, though highly criticized, the most important (Murray 1990).

As Murray's thesis is grounded upon a number of key assumptions about what an appropriate and healthy society is supposed to be, to understand his work it is necessary to consider what these are. In what may be regarded as an expression of a conventional conservative position, Murray idealizes the conventional heterosexual nuclear married family as the keystone around which healthy communities are established. This he considers the ideal family form, and he thinks this way because he believes that only this family unit can ensure the effective transmission of appropriate norms to its young. Though its role as a healthy socializing force is an important attribute of the success of the nuclear family, it is also functionally superior to other forms because it helps shape the personality structure of the adults within it in positive and productive law-abiding ways. Men, he believes, unless pacified and domesticated through marriage into such a family form, are likely to degenerate into something approaching a primal savage nature. As he argues:

> Just as work is more important than merely making a living, getting married and raising a family are more than just a way to pass the time. Supporting a family is a central means for a man to prove to himself that he is a 'mensch'. Men who do not support families find other ways to prove that they are men, which tend to take various destructive forms. As many have commentated through the centuries, young males are essentially barbarians for whom marriage – meaning not just the wedding vows, but the act of taking responsibility for a wife and children – is an indispensable civilising force. (Murray 1990)

A healthy and crime-free culture for Murray is one where the nuclear family form prevails as the norm and from which other family forms – particularly single-parent families – are noticeable by their absence. The young in such a context are socialized appropriately, not only because there are two parents available to socialize them, but also because the process of socialization requires the presence of a male role model. As far as Murray is concerned, this is a figure that can only be provided by the male head of the nuclear family. In other words, an on-site male parent. Women by implication, he argues, cannot provide the support young men require to fulfil this socialization role. Unless attached to a father, they remain an altogether inadequate agent of socialization.

Just as their involvement in families produces a healthy individual, so too does the involvement of males in paid work. It is a force of good in the world because, for Murray, it guarantees a stable adult personality. It provides males in particular with a sense of satisfaction in the world. It keeps them away from trouble, while also providing them with the material wealth they require in order to invest in hearth and home. Though celebrating the importance of paid work, Murray however appears to believe that it is the work ethic itself that is more important. In other words, a commitment to work is more significant than actually having it.

For a fully healthy culture to be sustained, a community must be constructed around a stable array of nuclear families to which their members are committed. This commitment is not only evidenced through belief in such things as the sanctity of marriage, but also by a sense of collectively felt disgust expressed by members towards more deviant family forms. These factors, acting in conjunction with a strong commitment to a work ethic, will lead men to undertake the work necessary to meet the material needs of their kith and kin. Finally, because the good community is made up of active fathers who are also around to support their young, a community of living role models is at hand to inspire their male offspring.

The problem with our present, at least according to Murray, is that the conditions that have traditionally led to the construction of orderly law-abiding communities have been systematically undermined by liberal welfare policy. This trend in social policy, evident above all in the rise of the postwar welfare state and its promulgation of a permissive social agenda, has, Murray contends, fatal consequences for the way in which social life for poor communities has evolved and developed.

With the rise of the permissive society, a commitment to the nuclear family has declined, while an acceptance of family types that depart from it has become widely accepted. No longer experiencing the shame that once discouraged permissive behaviour, young women engage in casual sex outside of marriage and sometimes do so in order to secure social housing for themselves and their illegitimate offspring. Excessive welfare, though directed with the aim of helping the urban poor, comes to betray its benevolent goal by producing a dependency culture while simultaneously eroding the work ethic. Left with no other goal in life, young men gather in the streets, thus setting in motion a process that leads to their mal-socialization into the skills that will equip them for involvement in crimes such as street robbery.

Instead of looking to support their families, young men engage in casual sex with permissive women and move on to repeat the same process with others. Unable to provide an adequate socializing force in a world where male fathers are no longer part of nuclear families, young women bring into the world an underclass of young males devoid of the moral consciousness that proper socialization provides. Lacking access to necessary role models, they are thus perfectly tailored, Murray argues, for a life of crime. Like their feckless parents, young men and women grow up in a world with the expectation that welfare provides all. Not having to bother with work, the young simply live off welfare provision. Having no goal in life, their turn to crime, at least for Murray, is a foregone conclusion.

In order to avoid the critique that his work simply criminalizes the poor, Murray – drawing upon an older Victorian tradition – distinguishes the working class into respectable and non-respectable elements. The former, while poor, at least marry into and remain committed to the nuclear family, while also manifesting a respectable orientation towards the Protestant work ethic. The latter do not, which justifies their designation as 'underclass'. While distinguishing the decent from the immoral poor, Murray's work not only provides an explanation of street crime in general, but also provides, controversially, an account of why young black males are disproportionately involved in offences such as street robbery. This follows logically from his conception of the single parent family as pathological. It so happens that within the black community a far higher number of single parent families can be found. The social equation for Murray is clear: absence of the father figure added to single mothers equals illegitimate offspring.

Though the effects of poor parenting feature significantly in new right of centre accounts of street robbery, the corrupting influences of illegal drug use and mass culture are also evoked to explain the production of the street robber.

Underpinning the first of these arguments is the assumption that the effects of drug use or the reality of addiction weaken moral constraints, leaving the individual concerned at the mercy of more primitive drives. This explanation considers involvement in acts such as street robbery to have occurred because the body is overwhelmed by too many of the wrong kind of chemicals, or as a result of the body's anguish at being denied the chemicals the addiction demands. Put more simply, the robber robs either because their drug of choice drives them to commit crime – because that is what drugs do, or in order to obtain the resources to sustain an addiction that cannot be paid for in any other way. Melanie Phillips puts the case in stark terms (though not by providing much in the way of hard evidence) in her consideration of the effects of marijuana use on the young:

> Several studies have found it can cause impulsively violent behaviour, and is associated with violent death. One study found a far higher mortality rate among cannabis users with a very high proportion of violent deaths. Out of 268 New Yorkers sent to prison in 1984 for murder, 73 were under the influence of cannabis at the time of their crime. (Phillips 2002)

The second corrupting influence often identified by the right concerns the individual's exposure to what is believed to be a degenerate and corrupting mass culture that sanctifies violence and which has appeared to have abandoned any commitment to traditional moral verities.[2] In their attempt to identify the culprits responsible for the production of this morally repugnant culture, the right have identified a number of suitable enemies. These include a Hollywood industry responsible for producing hyper-violent movies; TV channels (like Channel 4) which the right castigate for their alleged permissiveness; and, last but not least, popular music such as rap that consciously repudiates every moral standard the right believed a good society should embody. Melanie Phillips, again, summarizes this position well. Young poor men, she concludes, are:

> Increasingly unable to distinguish fantasy from reality, they are all too vulnerable to the popular culture of violence and sadism – murderous computer games, or 'gangsta rap' with its glamorising of guns, violence and hatred. (Phillips 2003)

That these corrupting forces are allowed to exist without serious censure presupposes – at least for the right – that there are a number of things wrong with the society that has encouraged such developments. For clearly and self-evidently, something had to be wrong with society for a situation to occur in which young people were being exposed to such a corrupting set of influences. In their attempt to identify the deeper causes of street robbery, the right have typically identified as a principal determinant the failure of existing informal and formal social control measures. To establish the precise relation of this causal factor to street robbery, this argument suggests that acts like robbery are encouraged because there is a surfeit of the wrong kind of control and a deficit in the forms of control and regulation that might prevent it. Who then is to blame for this state of affairs?

On this matter, commentators of the right have identified a number of internal enemies. These include a liberal/left intelligentsia they consider responsible for promulgating and encouraging a destructive permissive approach to life, and those who, by creating a liberal welfare state, ensured that these destructive ideas were then translated into social policy – a critique at the heart of Murray's underclass thesis. These forces, they suggest, are guilty precisely because they have encouraged ways of life that directly undermine the moral fabric of the good society, while emasculating the kind of robust controls that might have prevented this moral lapse to begin with. By encouraging a lax moral culture, so the preconditions have been created for the emergence of young men tailor-made for a life of crime. At the same time, by failing to ensure that appropriate social controls are supported, so the good society is left exposed to the criminals that an immoral culture would produce. In response to this state of affairs, the right have called for much more severe punishment, more imprisonment and a reorientation of the criminal justice system in ways that will offer more benefits to the victim and to the victimized public.

Critique

So far we have considered the various factors that right of centre commentators have adduced to explain why certain people turn to street robbery. In what follows I will present a critical overview of this position. Is it a fair and accurate representation of the factors that lead to street crime, and if it is not, in which respects is it wrong? In developing this critique, I will address not so much the work of particular theorists, so much as the general propositions that underpin right of centre thinking as a whole. In so doing my aim will be to answer the following questions, each of which problematizes a fundamental plank in the argument developed by the right:

1   Does the deficit model of the street robber accord with what we know about street robbers?
2   How pathological is the parent culture that is typically held responsible for producing the street robber as a motivated offender?
3   Is liberalism really to blame for encouraging the pathological developments within poor communities that give birth to the street robber?

The first point to be made when considering the deficit model of the criminal articulated by the right is that it is by no means a new way of looking at what is, after all, an old problem. If we return to the historical record and consider, for example, how the Victorians considered their own street robbers then one conclusion that can be reached with some certainty is that not much has changed between then and now. Writing in 1839, W.A. Miles had no problem connecting rising crime in London (as we saw in chapter 2) with what he identified as a criminal underclass he depicted graphically as 'a race *sui generis*. A race, he claimed, that was 'different from the rest of society not only in thoughts, habits and manners, but even in appearance' (Miles 1839). Writing in the same vein in 1849, Thomas Beggs also had no problem identifying the criminal classes with 'veriest debasement'. They yielded, he argued, 'obedience only to the animal instincts; brooding in the spiritual darkness in a day of gospel light' (Beggs 1849). The tone may be different from that deployed by Murray, but the idea of a criminal fraternity constructed in terms of essentualized difference is very much the same.

Just as populist commentators on the right today highlight the contaminating impact of violent mass culture upon the street criminal, so too did the Victorians who, like Mayhew, believed terrible moral consequences would befall those exposed to it. Remarking on the debilitating impact of the halfpenny romances on the London poor, Mayhew indignantly observed: 'One of the worst of the newest ones is denominated "Charley Wagg, or the New Jack Shepherd, a history of the most successful thief in London." To say that they are not incentives to lust, theft and crime is to cherish a fallacy' (Mayhew 1861 (1985)).

But what status ought we to concede to this kind of explanation. Is the robber really as different as the right suggest. To answer this question we need as a precursor to attend to what offenders actually have to say. This, it could be pointed out, is not something that many commentators on the right have chosen to do. Under the dead weight of presumption, offenders' testimonies are largely absent from consideration.

As part of the interview research I conducted among young street robbers in Lambeth, I sought to rectify this deficit by asking them a series of questions designed to see just how aware they were of the moral status of the offences they had committed. I did so to test the claim we find inherent in the deficit approach to the offender which suggests that what we are dealing with is a hardened predator devoid of moral consciousness. To examine this issue I asked the offenders whether they viewed what they had done as wrong. The first point that could be made was that all of them recognized clearly that they had broken rules and that what they had done was morally reprehensible. They could, in other words, tell right from wrong. What their testimonies indicated was not only that most had internalized a moral consciousness, but also that it was a well-developed one. As one interviewee put it: 'I know I was a bad boy'.

All accepted that the police were right to have apprehended them and they also accepted, albeit with a sense of pragmatic acquiescence, the right of society to punish them for what they had done. To this extent it was evident that they had internalized a series of dominant norms that condemned rule-breaking. When pushed further, it was also evident that most possessed some sense of a moral universe. In form, this moral world-view often approximated a version of Kantianism. This was reflected in the belief often echoed by the offenders interviewed of their desire to live in a world in which the moral imperative of doing unto others as you would have them do unto you should hold sway and prosper.

The capacity of street robbers actively to identify with many of the values of the dominant society they prey upon, in particular its materialist culture, also supports the idea that they are not simply a predatory outsider totally devoid of what law-abiding people possess. Indeed, as Sykes and Matza observed many years ago: 'While supposedly thoroughly committed to the deviant system of the delinquent subculture, he [the deviant] would appear to recognise the moral validity of the dominant normative system in many instances' (Sykes 1957). Returning to the research conducted with young offenders, the truth of this observation came through repeatedly. None saw themselves as career criminals and most had a future exit strategy that typically involved passing exams and getting a job. While they had clearly 'drifted' into crime in Matza's sense of this term, all saw their future in the formal economy. What I took from this was the observation that, for most of the street robbers I interviewed, street robbery was not a place they wished to remain, but was simply another temporary and unstable job in a world where good jobs were largely absent.

As we saw above, integral to the conservative conception of the street robber was an individual conceived as in effect out of control, at the mercy of primary drives and seemingly unshackled from the benevolent impact of civilizing forces. While this representation of the robber corresponds well to a conventional common-sense view of the criminal as a dangerous other, there is little evidence from the research conducted with offenders that this conception has any basis in reality. This is particularly evident if we consider the thesis that robbery was being perpetrated because those involved had a drug problem. This hypothesis, circulated widely by the right-wing media, and accepted by many police commentators and, not least, by government ministers, presents a potent image of the robber as essentially someone out of control and at the mercy of more primary drives. If true, this hypothesis would apparently explain a lot. Drugs, after all, do strange things to people, and those with an addiction are driven by it to commit all kinds of unspeakable acts … aren't they? Well not in the case of the street robber.

Again, from the interviews I conducted with young street robbers – and this is replicated in other research (Kershaw 2001; Fitzgerald *et al.* 2002) – there is no evidence at all to suggest either that drug use stimulates the desire to rob or that growing drug use explains the recent rise in street robbery. Indeed, when I brought this issue up in interviews conducted with young offenders, one common reaction was outright incredulity in the face of the suggestion. These young men, aged between 15 and 19, were very conscious of their bodies and had clearly bought into the myth of the body beautiful. Their physical prowess evident both in the ability to be able to handle themselves in the event of trouble and not least avoid what they viewed as the lumpen efforts of overweight police officers to catch them, was very important to their self-image as virile males. This did not mean that they did not use drugs, but what it did mean was that what they did use was for recreational purposes and was not directly connected with street crime. To this extent, like many young people in British society, they were part of a generation who had been well and truly socialized into a society where drug use had become normalized. Marijuana appeared in most cases to be their preferred drug of choice. When I asked them what they thought of heavy drug users such as heroin addicts, what I discovered was that for these young men this was by far their most despised category of being. They were, in their estimation, a category they considered the lowest of the low. As one young man stated when I asked him whether he (and other street robbers he knew) used crack he was adamant that 'it's not us'. He went on: 'the people what uses it are like tramps and so forth'.

The fallacy of this kind of 'explanation' is also well illustrated by the application of common sense. To perpetrate street robbery well you have to have your wits about you. You have to move quickly and think on your feet. Being 'stoned', 'out of your box', or addled on crack cocaine or heroin does not kit you out well for this role. Street robbers are well aware of this. So indeed are heroin addicts, which is one reason they rarely engage in street robbery.

In summary, it could be said that while it is evident that young people who commit street robbery are certainly individuals who commit immoral acts, their engagement in street robbery does not follow on from the idea that they have no moral sensibilities. Nor are they at the mercy of primitive drives because they are in some respect 'out of control' because of their drug use.

Let us now turn to the next two planks in the argument proposed by the right and consider, firstly, just how pathological the parent culture is into which the street robber is allegedly born, and secondly, assess how far its pathologies are created by liberal tendencies at work in the welfare state. To begin with, what evidence is there to suggest that people who perpetrate street robbery do so because they have been mal-socialized as a consequence of their exposure to workshy parents mired in permissiveness and addicted to a dependency culture?

If we consider what other studies of crime among working-class communities have to tell us, a number of serious objections could be directed against this line of argument.

In a recent attempt to study the social background of those who engage in street robbery, Fitzgerald et al. found little evidence to suggest that robbers were the products of a malformed and maladjusted underclass (Fitzgerald et al. 2002). What their work indicates is a background culture characterized by what they liken to serious patterns of social disorganization. What their study brought to light was a world of highly stressed individuals, particularly single parents, attempting to do right in a hostile social and economic context. It is poor living conditions acting in conjunction with a highly restricted access to the labour market that, they argue, produces the conditions that foster the kind of street life and street culture that can and will result in street robbery.

This analysis, it must be emphasized, does not deny the fact that certain young people will indeed find themselves – as the right argue – mixing with street cultures that can encourage involvement in street robbery. Where this analysis departs radically from the right, however, is by suggesting that the social forces that create the preconditions for this do not emanate from cultural failings among working-class populations but from the socio-economic failings of free-market capitalism. The problem for writers such as Murray is that they do not want to recognize the fundamental importance of these issues. The role of unemployment and underemployment, for example, have no explanatory status in Murray's account, nor does he adequately attend to the changing economy of British society, even though it has changed significantly and with profound consequences on issues such as street robbery – a point I will pick up on in the next chapter.

With regards to the claim that society is too lenient and that there are no effective deterrents available to discourage young people from crime, three points can be made against it. To begin with, it is important to note that the overwhelming majority of those aged 19 or over successfully convicted of a street robbery offence *will* receive a custodial sentence. If you are black and live in areas like Brixton, this percentage is higher than if you are a white street robber. Sentences are also routinely meted out even if the robbery was a first-time offence. Indeed, from evidence collated from Lambeth (Hallsworth and Richie 2002) you were more likely to receive a harsher sentence for robbery than you would for assault. The idea that Britain is 'soft' in relation to the way it deals with street robbers is one of those ongoing myths the right habitually seeks to sustain – despite the availability of evidence proving the contrary.

Having examined the arguments that right of centre commentators have adduced to explain street robbery, it is clear that they offer explanations that can be criticized on many fronts. The evidential basis remains weak and the deficit model of crime at the heart of right thinking remains highly problematic. Shorn of hard evidence, what we find is less an appropriate account of street robbery, and more a series of persecution texts directed at blaming poor communities for the crime that bedevils social life within them. If the right fails to address the problem of street robbery, however, can commentators of the political left fare any better?

Notes

1 For examples of this see Jenson, A. (1969). 'How Much Can we Boost IQ and Scholastic Achievement?' *Harvard Educational Review* 39: 1–123.A.; Herrenstein, R. and Murray, C. (1994) *The Bell Curve: Intelligence and Class Structure in American Life.* New York and London: Free Press. For a contemporary critique, see Bowling, B. and Phillips, C. (2002) *Racism, Crime and Justice.* London: Longman.
2 See Wartella, B. (1995) 'Media and Problem Behaviours in Young People' in *Psychological Disorders in Young People*, D.S.M. Rutter. London: Wiley: 296–323. For an overview of this literature, see Reiner, R. (1997) 'Media Made Criminality' in *Oxford Handbook of Criminology*, R.M.M. Maguire and R. Reiner. Oxford: Oxford University Press.

Chapter 5

The view from the left

While commentators on the political right have exhibited little hesitation in identifying the factors they believe explain street crime, the left has demonstrated little appetite for engaging in the hunt for causal explanations in quite the same way. Indeed, if we consider how the left has addressed the problem of street robbery, it could be observed that, while it has produced highly sophisticated accounts of corporate crime and youth subculture, the same cannot be said of its approach to this perennial offence category. Three reasons can be cited to explain this sorry state of affairs. Firstly, as an offence that typically involves poor people preying on other poor people, the street robber has not provided the left with much that could sanction any meaningful politics of recognition. Secondly, when robbery has been considered worthy of analysis, explanations for it typically appear subsumed within more general theories of working-class crime. Finally, instead of explaining why certain populations become engaged in robbery, the left has often preferred to study the disproportionate social response this offence provokes. As this hesitation on the part of the left is itself of interest to this study, I will examine these factors in more detail. Though the tenor of this examination will remain critical, I will also suggest that, despite its hesitation, the left has made a number of important observations about street robbery that any comprehensive theory worthy of its name will need to accept and build upon.

The first reason that may be cited to explain the hesitation on the part of the left to engage with street robbery can be attributed to the fact that it did not constitute an offence that the left could portray at all sympathetically. It was and remains an offence disproportionately perpetrated by poor people and, by and large, the population of victims are also poor. As Young observes:

> Street crime is the only form of serious crime where the victim is in the same social category as the offender. It is lower working class against lower working class, black against black and neighbour against neighbour. Much of it represents the ultimate in anti-social behaviour and unites all sections of the population against a common enemy. (Young 1979)

Unlike the array of flamboyant subcultures that emerged in postwar Britain – held up by the left as exemplifying resistance to a deeply inequitable and class-divided society – it is difficult to categorize street crime in quite the same way (Hebdige 1979). For a tradition whose political standpoint was forged through an attempt to resist the criminalizing tendencies of the state, the modern street robber would not provide much that would sanction any meaningful politics of recognition. Indeed, for a tradition that had traditionally sought, as Cohen describes it, to 'humanise the deviant' (Cohen 1981), the street robber did not constitute a deviant that many found worthy of 'humanising'.

This reluctance to endorse the street robber, it could be noted, is by no means new. Indeed, it represents a standpoint whose genesis can be traced back to the nineteenth century, where it is writ large in the work of Marx and Engels. For them the street robber was simply a member of the lumpen proletariat; an 'underclass' that existed by preying parasitically upon other disadvantaged working-class people (Engels). Far from conceiving the robber as a 'social bandit', as Marxist historians have sought to do (Hobsbawn 2000), the left has preferred instead to conceive in this figure an unfortunate and condensed expression of the barbarities capitalist society invariably induces (Platt 1978).

If anger and embarrassment may be cited as an important reason why the left has failed to study street robbery, it has been compounded in recent years by another. At stake here is the contentious issue of race, and, in particular, the way the political right has seized upon what it claims amounts to black over-representation in street robbery. Though the left has never denied the fact that minority ethnic groups have been involved in crime, many remain convinced – for reasons we shall examine in more detail below – that the coverage given to their involvement remains vastly disproportionate to the threat allegedly identified. Indeed, far from engaging in an objective reporting of 'facts', what really underlies such reporting, Gilroy argues, is no more than a racist agenda set upon proving that the black population is inherently criminogenic and poses by its presence a serious threat to the white population and the British way of life.

As critical criminology emerged, not least to resist the racializing agenda of the right, it was from the beginning unprepared to endorse a research agenda that would appear to concede legitimacy to what Gilroy would term the 'myth' of black criminality (Gilroy 1987). To do so, it was felt, would be to reproduce the dangerous reification of 'black crime' while also marking out the black population as a suspect community for yet more coercive regulation and control. This standpoint, it could be noted, has become something of orthodoxy for the critical left, and its sway still remains intact – up to the present day[1] – a point I will return to below.

The left's failure to address street robbery with the kind of panache it reserved for youth subcultures also follows through from the perception that, all things considered, it was not a particularly complicated offence or one that required its own unique theory to explain. As far as offences go, it remains, after all, on the lowest rung of any hierarchy of crime; while, as a crime perpetrated by the poor, its persistence in capitalist societies was held to be unproblematically connected with the disadvantages the poor confront. Considered this way, street robbery has been traditionally conceived as simply an emergent feature of the structural inequalities always present within a capitalist mode of production (Platt 1978). Capitalism, after all, invariably produces disadvantage, and disadvantage in capitalism will invariably provoke adaptations that lead to offences such as street crime. The seemingly straightforward obviousness of this equation, I would suggest, has resulted in a tradition that has not really felt the need to enquire comprehensively into street robbery as an offence. What it has sought to do instead, is either to prove statistically the relation between inequality, deprivation and involvement in crime, and to demonstrate that rising crime among the urban poor is connected to changes in the social structure of capitalist society in the postwar period. Fitzgerald *et al.*'s (2002) work on the social conditions behind contemporary street robbery which we considered in the previous chapter exemplify this kind of research tradition. The problem is either one of deprivation, poverty or exclusion (Box 1987), or rising patterns of relative deprivation (Young 1984).

The final reason that can be adduced to explain why the left has failed to provide detailed accounts of street robbery follows through from the assumption that the social attention directed towards this offence is not justified by its seriousness. When compared, for example, with the crimes of the powerful, street robbery occasions far less material harm to society, a fact powerfully illustrated in a study conducted by Snider who estimated that while the annual cost of street crime in the USA came to a figure of some $4 billion, this was less than 5 per cent of the amount lost through corporate crime (Winslow 2003). Despite the social and material costs posed to society by crimes perpetrated by the powerful, however, it is also evident that their acts receive less attention and certainly far less censure than the crimes committed by the poor. At the same time, it is also evident that, while they occasion far less harm, offences like street robbery receive a disproportionate amount of media and political attention.

Given the costs of corporate crime but the silence that surrounds it, and given the saturation coverage accorded to working-class crime despite the relatively low scale of harm it occasions, critical criminologists have responded in two very different ways. On the one hand, a growing number have begun to rectify this research deficit by drawing attention back to the crimes of the powerful and away from the traditional focus of criminology upon working-class crime (Croall 1992). Others, however, have begun to examine in far greater detail precisely why relatively low-status offences such as street crime came to assume such a significant role on the public agenda.

Though the left has not conceded to the study of street robbery the same kind of attention it has reserved for other forms of crime, it is nevertheless the case that the single most influential text on street robbery in postwar criminology was composed within this tradition. The text in question was *Policing the Crisis: Mugging, the State, Law and Order,* written in 1978 by Stuart Hall, Chas Critcher, Tony Jefferson, John Clarke and Brian Roberts of the Birmingham School of Cultural Studies. As this text exemplifies a conventional left position on street robbery, in what follows I will consider its central arguments before subjecting the position of the left as a whole to critique.

Policing the Crisis

Policing the Crisis was written as a critical analysis of street robbery and, in particular, the moral panic that surrounded it during 1970–72 in the UK, a period during which the urban black 'mugger' first made his appearance in Britain. The text begins with an examination and then a critical demolition of the evidential basis that the media deployed to justify the selective and sensational attention they gave to street crime during this period. The newsworthiness of street crime, Hall *et al.*

argued, could not be explained in terms of a sharp and unexpected rise in this crime category, because the empirical evidence simply did not support this interpretation. Street crime, they argued, was an old offence whose rate and incidence had not changed significantly over time. Nor could media and political interest in street crime be explained in terms of an old crime now being perpetrated in new ways. The expression 'mugging', which the media quickly latched upon to describe street crime during this period, was not, Hall *et al.* argued, a statutory offence; and, far from describing a new offence or offender (Phillips 2003), was simply a new label for an existing array of offences. The response to street crime did not, as a consequence, appear warranted by the reality.

In their attempt to make sense of the sensational reporting street robbery received at the hands of the media, Hall *et al.* drew upon a concept first developed by Cohen in his influential study of the social response to Mods and Rockers in the 1960s (Cohen 1980). What the media had generated, they argued, was a 'moral panic'.

> When the official reaction to a person, groups of persons or series of events is out of all proportion to the actual threat offered, when 'experts' in the form of police chiefs, the judiciary, politicians and editors perceive the threat in all but identical terms and appear to talk with one voice of rates, diagnosis, prognosis and solutions, when the media representations universally stress 'sudden and dramatic increases' (in numbers involved or events) and 'novelty' above and beyond what a sober, realistic appraisal could sustain, then we believe it appropriate to speak of the beginnings of a moral panic. (Hall *et al.* 1978)

What they then sought to explain was how and why this moral panic around mugging had appeared when the facts did not by 'sober, realistic appraisal' justify the attention it had received. As empirical facts about street robbery could not provide them with an answer to this question, their focus shifted towards accounting for the social response itself. From looking at the deviant act – the conventional focus of criminological enquiry – they refocussed instead upon 'the relation between the deviant act and the reaction of the public and control agencies to the act' (Hall *et al.* 1978).

To accomplish this task, they began by assiduously studying the genesis of the moral panic, paying particular attention to the way in which the mugging label came into popular usage during this period and was then subsequently applied. As their research demonstrated, prior to the 1970s the term mugging had no history of use in postwar Britain. It was, however, a term routinely used by commentators in the US to describe street robbery. What the British media had done, Hall *et al.* argued, was to adopt this term to describe what they then claimed was in the process of happening on Britain's inner-city streets.

What was imported, however, was far more than a new description of an old offence. For in this American import, what was being appropriated was a label to which an assemblage of already existing references and associations were attached. The mugging label thus came contextualized and racialized when the media began to apply it in a 'scene-setting' manner to help to explain events in a British context. As Hall *et al.* note:

> 'Mugging' comes to Britain first as an American phenomenon, but fully thematised and contextualised. It is embedded in a number of linked frames: the race conflict, the urban crisis, rising crime, the breakdown of law and order; the liberal conspiracy and the white backlash. It is no mere fact about crime that is reported. It connotes a whole historical construction about the nature and dilemmas of American society. (Hall *et al.* 1978)

When the British media began to deploy the term mugging to define what they claimed was happening on the streets of Britain, they did so against a background characterized by economic decline, and not least the breakdown of the postwar welfare state settlement. It was at this moment that the black community, already one of the poorest and most economically marginalized populations in British society, found itself singled out for special treatment. This revealed itself, Hall *et al.* argue, in a movement that would see black communities in general and young black males in particular subjected to an undeclared urban war by the police, the active agents of a deeply repressive and racist state.

By the time the moral panic over rising street crime had begun, Hall *et al.* argued, this urban war was already well under way. Young black males were finding themselves subject to racialized targeting by the police, while the areas in which they lived were subject to highly intensive and coercive policing. It is in this context that an articulation between police activity, media coverage and street crime activity began to be forged. The robbers provided the facts; well-reported police arrests confirmed them; and both street crime and the response towards it provided a context the media then began to interpret by reference to the mugging label it had imported from the US.

A robbery initiated in Handsworth by three black youths on an elderly white victim was widely reported in the mass media during this period. This provided the focal point around which events on the ground and its discursive representation would coalesce. The robbery was used to suggest, not only that there was a crisis of law and order in the UK, but also that Britain was sliding inexorably in the same direction as America. By 'cashing in on Handsworth', the media were also able to highlight and identify the population that would henceforth be identified as the principal perpetrators behind the crisis: young black males living in inner-city areas. The Handsworth case was also used to confirm the identity of the victims: a defenceless white society.

As the moral panic subsequently unfolded, the primary definers of the crisis – which now included politicians and members of the judiciary, as well as police sources and journalists – began to accept the terms implied by the mugging label. By so doing, they came to speak with one voice about what was represented as a law and order crisis accepted as having a common cause. Such convergence, however, did not require a conspiracy for it to be accomplished. All the participants simply quoted each other and used the testimony of others to reinforce their own position. The press used police statistics, and quoted from judges and politicians whose understanding of the street crime problem was also informed by the media. And so the moral panic escalated.

In creating the definitional space, a number of key themes gradually coalesced in the way that the mugging 'crisis' was being constructed. Under the impact of the label, crime in general and street robbery in particular became racialized in a new and sinister way. The street robber would henceforth always now be considered to have a black face, just as the victim population would invariably be presented as white. In the face of such attention, crime became racialized while the black population found itself and its culture further criminalized. It came to be seen, in effect, as a dangerous predator that posed by its presence a direct threat, not only to white victims, but also to a British way of life represented as essentially law-abiding. Mugging, was something new, something that was morally reprehensible, and, as such, un-English and intolerable.

The alleged escalation in mugging was also deployed as a critique of current social control mechanisms. In this context, conservative commentators used it to draw attention to what was presented as the bankruptcy of liberal, welfare-state solutions to crime. This was demonstrated both by the failure of the system to curtail the crisis of escalating violence, and by its complicity in creating the conditions of lawless promiscuity that allowed it to thrive. From this definition of the mugging problem, advocating hard-line repressive law and order solutions followed logically as the only suitable solution to the crisis. It was specifically within this definitional consensus that the government of the time began to initiate the steps necessary to defend what the media had construed as a defenceless society. Police powers were increased; more resources were targeted towards policing lawless inner-city areas; and the judiciary played its part by handing down disproportionately harsh punitive sentences to street robbers.

For Hall *et al.* it was not rising rates of street robbery that provoked the social response it received in any causally direct way. On the contrary, the sensational media attention it received had to be understood in terms of the political economy of postwar British society and the power relations that defined it. The concluding sections of the book seek to establish this connection.

By the 1970s Britain's postwar boom economy had tilted into recession, heralding a process of sustained decline. One consequence of this would be to demonstrate visibly Britain's diminished status as an imperial world power. In the face of a burgeoning economic crisis that would see mass industrial unrest, three-day weeks and eventually the destruction of vast sections of primary manufacturing industries, the class consensus that had been established in the postwar period was in the process of collapsing. The extension of workers' rights, the formation of a welfare state and attempts to initiate corporatist solutions to industrial problems – all of which had underpinned the postwar welfare settlement – no longer worked to secure ruling-class power and thus ensure its domination or 'hegemony', as Hall *et al.* (drawing upon the work of the Italian Marxist Gramsci) defined it. What resulted was what they termed an 'organic crisis of the state'. This term defined a situation characterized by the failure of the ruling class to ensure the reproduction of the conditions of their rule through imposing intellectual and moral domination.

It is precisely at this point in time – when hegemony was failing – that the moral panic around mugging began to surface. The conjunction was by no means accidental. What it would facilitate would be a way of resolving the organic crisis of the state both by helping forge a new social consensus and, by so doing, help reconstruct hegemonic equilibrium in British society. It would function this way because in its identification of the black mugger, a convenient folk devil was identified upon which the collected fury of British society could be mobilized and projected. Different classes might well be opposed in every other respect, but in the face of the mugging crime wave a common point of consensus would be reached. The mugger, in other words, could and would provide a point of negative identification around which a consensus could be established. A disunited society would become united in their hatred and condemnation of the mugger, and all classes would accept the law and order solutions proposed by the state as a just and necessary 'solution' to the crisis.

In a world where adult fears about unruly youth already had currency, and where a legacy of institutionalized racism already existed, the young black urban male appeared tailor-made for the scapegoating role he would now be expected to perform. What the moral panic was able to achieve was a reconstruction of Britain's economic and political crisis as essentially a crisis of law and order, seemingly solvable only through the judicious advocation of law and order solutions. In this scapegoating process, the black mugger was positioned not only as a folk devil upon which society's fury could be projected, but also as a functional prop that could be deployed to help the state 'police the crisis' in ways that prevented the real economic causes from becoming visible. This it would achieve by, in effect, displacing attention from the economic base (the real cause of the crisis) and relocating it directly onto the ideological superstructure, where it was discursively constructed as a crisis of law and order. In this act of ideological displacement, the foundations were laid for what would become a new hegemonic equilibrium that would itself involve the genesis of a new state form. What it would permit would be the formation of what, following Poulantzas, Hall *et al.* would identify as an exceptional 'authoritarian state' and the forward 'drift' into what Hall would subsequently describe as the formation of a 'law and order society' (Hall 1980). This, then, is what the politics of street crime was really about – the manufacture of consent in class-divided societies by authoritarian means.

Though *Policing the Crisis* was written principally as an attempt to study the relation between the deviant act (mugging) and the social response it produced, the text does contain, specifically towards its end, an account of the deviant act itself which it also seeks to explain. Though this explanation is posed very much as a supplementary narrative which by no means sits easily with the initial research focus, it is worth considering because it does express a typical conception of street crime and the street criminal as conceived within Marxist criminology.

Whereas Marx and Engels (as we have seen) considered the 'criminal classes' within capitalist society as a depoliticized 'lumpen proletariat', this view is not the one adopted by the authors of *Policing the Crisis*. Far from being external to the working class, the black urban street robber came from and belonged to its most hyper-exploited faction. Forced into a situation of wagelessness and consequently unemployment and underemployment, the black population endured systematic expulsion from productive labour. This pattern of economic marginalization was also reinforced, Hall *et al.* argue, by spatial compression into the ghetto and by the endemic racism the black population confront at every level in British society.

Given their harsh and brutal location within British society, the preconditions were established for the emergence of a number of different survival strategies on the part of this hyper-exploited population. To meet their material needs, some young men embraced 'hustling cultures' or turned towards crime, while others dramatized their exclusion through embracing subcultures of resistance such as reggae and Rastafarianism. Though different in form, what unified these cultural adaptations was a common recognition that the destiny of the black population in Britain was not to fulfil the role capital had ascribed to them as a reserve army of labour. A population, that is, to be drawn on for low-grade productive work in times of economic upturn; or as a population whose unemployment could be productively deployed to keep wages low.

The involvement of young black males in street crime, while a negative adaptation to their situation, is at the same time an act which is also entirely comprehensible, as it is rooted in the material reality in which many members of the black population are forced to exist. In other words, street crime arises not only because of *economic want*, but because there is a *political refusal* on the part of many young blacks to become deskilled labour consigned to a life of doing 'white man's shit work'. The causal factors at play here are therefore both *economic* and *ideological* in form (Hall *et al.* 1978). The turn to crime, while comprehensible and understandable, nevertheless produces the conditions necessary for the reconstruction of hegemony and the formation of a 'law and order society'. For in responding to their plight through street robbery, the black sub-proletariat implicitly sanctions the state with the justification it requires for engaging in its punitive turn. By engaging in crime as a rational response to its predicament, the black population justified its reconstruction as an internal enemy that would require the coercive regulation and control meted out to it.

Critique

Having studied how the left has approached the issues posed by street robbery, what lessons can be learnt? To answer this question I will begin by reconsidering the reasons why left of centre commentators have often proved hesitant to study street robbery. This is necessary because, as I will argue, their silence remains a problem. I will then consider the status of the explanations that critical criminologists have adduced to explain street robbery and the social response it has provoked. Despite their hesitation to study street robbery, the left offers, I will suggest, a far more plausible account of street robbery than the deficit models of the right.

As we observed above, the left's hesitation to engage in street robbery was motivated by what appear to be at first sight a number of seemingly admirable reasons. If an admirable set of intentions informs this position there remain, however, a number of serious problems with this standpoint that also need to be recognized.

The first criticism was made a number of years ago by Young, when he argued that by not attending to the crimes of the poor the left had literally conceded the law and order agenda to the right, who had no trouble engaging in such debates (Young 1997). Working-class people, after all, do commit crime and their victims are also drawn from the working-class communities upon whom they prey. Surveys on fear of crime, moreover, also suggest that street robbery is perceived as a serious problem by local communities. Indeed, when asked to list which problem they considered most acute in the area where they lived, the respondents to a community safety survey conducted in Lambeth in 2002 overwhelmingly selected street crime. Nor can this be considered a choice made in bad faith or because the population was in some way ideologically mystified. Given the high prevalence of this offence in Lambeth, it could be remarked that their choice was by no means an irrational one.

While commentators like Gilroy and Keith are right to highlight the criminalizing logic that often accompanies the way in which the black population has been treated, their argument that studies of black involvement in crime invariably reproduce the myth of black crime is itself a myth that left of centre politics would do well to disregard. While accepting that the coverage of black crime is often informed by a racialized agenda, it does not follow that all explanations of black people's involvement in crime are invariably racist. Nor should arguments about the potentially racist way in which explanations of black involvement in crime could be used justify not examining this issue. Surely at stake here is the explanatory power of the research initiated, and not least its integrity. Moreover, by not studying issues of criminal involvement by some members in the black community, I would suggest that minority ethnic groups are themselves dealt a disservice by those who claim to represent them. In a world where some young black men do become involved in street robbery, and in the context of a state that is all too ready to distribute disproportionate punishment to them, knowing why these young men become involved is surely of great significance.

While the reluctance of the left to engage fully with the issues raised by street robbery is indeed a problem, this has not prevented the left from making an important series of contributions to the study of this offence. In contrast to the deficit model of criminal involvement promoted by the right (considered in the previous chapter), those promoted by the left do offer the basis of a more sophisticated approach for making sense of street robbery. There are four positive lessons in particular that any explanation that claims comprehensiveness must bear in mind.

To begin with, the left is right to draw attention to the relationship between social class, class disadvantage and involvement in street robbery. Second, theorists of the left are also correct in suggesting that street robbery is a form of adaptation to the experience of deprivation in a class-divided society. Third, in arguing this case they are also correct in suggesting that to understand street robbery it is important to situate its analysis within a wider consideration of the political economy of the capitalist society in which it occurs. Street robbery, in other words, cannot simply be considered as a product of mal-socialized individuals, as underclass thinking imagines. On the contrary, its roots lie within the way society is itself organized. Finally, as Hall *et al.*'s work demonstrates, the social response to street robbery is never simply conditioned by the scale of its seriousness. There is always a politics at play in the attention it receives that needs to be recognized.

While the focus on disadvantage and its relation to street robbery is important, it is nevertheless also important to recognize that the relation between disadvantage and involvement in street robbery is by no means direct. Many, after all, are disadvantaged but do not engage in street robbery. To explain why some people and not others become involved in street robbery requires a theoretical approach that needs to move beyond stark notions of adaptations such as 'political refusal'. It not least requires articulating Mertonian ideas of adaptation with notions of what Sutherland terms 'differential association' in order to make sense of the complex mediations involved in the movement from an objective experience of deprivation (absolute or relative) and the decision to become involved in street robbery.

As we saw in our consideration of the deficit models of the right, integral to such accounts was a consideration of street robbers (both as individuals and as members of an underclass) as people fundamentally lacking what normal people were thought to possess. A similar kind of critique could also be made in relation to those who, like Hall *et al.*, also appear to consider the street robber as utterly excluded from mainstream society. For what left-orientated notions of exclusion posed in this manner often fail to see is precisely how far the street robber is also a product of the society whose members they attempt to rob. They are not essentially different even and despite their exclusion. As I will demonstrate in the chapters that follow, much of what motivates engagement in street robbery occurs not because street robbers are excluded from society but, on the contrary, from their successful internalization of its value system. In particular, the need to have and possess desirable material goods.

Finally, where the kind of explanation advanced by Hall *et al.* remains limited is in its focus on criminal involvement from the perspective of an analysis that considers the principal relationship to be between the street robber (and his political refusal) and the capitalist state that does the excluding. What such a position overlooks is a truth articulated well by proponents of control theory (Cohen 1979; Clarke 1980), which is to show that criminal involvement is also always about opportunity and issues of guardianship. After all, if the social controls directed to ensure the prevention of criminal behaviour were successful, it follows that street robbers would not continue to rob given the overwhelming likelihood of detection and prosecution. The lesson to be taken from this observation is that while control structures directed by the state to prevent robbery may indeed and often are repressive, this does not mean they are necessarily successful. It is consequently important to assess their deficiencies if we are to understand why street robbery occurs and at times rises.

Having considered in the previous two chapters the ways in which both right and left have addressed the issue of street robbery, the next chapter examines, on the basis of the critique developed in these chapters, how a more fully social theory of this offence can be constructed.

Note

1 For a recent example in this genre, see Bowling, B. and Phillips, C. (2002) *Racism, Crime and Justice*. London: Longman.

Chapter 6

Towards a framework of analysis

In Chapter 3 I considered the empirical data on street robbery in order to identify, as it were, the 'facts' of street robbery: who precisely is doing what to whom and where. In chapters 4 and 5 I considered how different theoretical traditions sought to account for these facts. In this chapter my aim will be to develop a framework for an analysis of contemporary street robbery that will build upon the critique developed in these chapters. The three chapters that follow will make an attempt to apply this framework to understand street crime in its contemporary context.

As we saw in the previous two chapters, there is no single agreed approach that can be adduced to explain why some people engage in street robbery. The world is rather characterized by a number of often mutually incompatible criminological approaches. The question such diversity poses is which approach do we adopt? To help answer this there are, I would suggest, three criteria we can apply to adjudicate upon the various categories of explanation on offer. First, the approach selected must be able to accommodate and explain all the trends identified in Chapter 3. Second, it must also be confirmed by reference to the available evidence. Third, it must recognize the complexity of the events it is trying to describe and explain. By applying this rule to the approaches considered in the previous two chapters, it is evident that many fail either because they are speculations which are not supported by empirical evidence, or involve conjectures that misinterpret the available evidence in important ways.

Those that fall foul of these criteria include accounts that explain robbery by reference to some notion of an inherent deficiency on the part of offenders, or which attribute its rise to variables such as drug use, or an underclass. Such accounts fail because the evidence does not support the conjecture advanced to explain the problem. Nor does the available evidence support a more radical interpretation of the street robber as someone who has been excluded from society. As we have seen, the desire of the street criminal for the very goods society itself classifies as desirable suggests a level of incorporation incommensurate with this perspective.

Even when the focus of analysis does offer some insight into why street crime occurs, such accounts are methodologically limited in terms of the explanations they advance because the focus of enquiry is too narrow and in its restriction it ignores the complexity of what it is trying to explain. The problem here is that the complexity of the world is lost in accounts which seek to advance an explanation premised upon the search for a single monolithic cause – be this the pathological implications of a dependency culture, or the hyper-exploitation inherent in late-modern racialized capitalist societies.

Rather than identify a monolithic cause and assert that this explains everything, in what follows I will begin with the assumption that street robbery (like all crime) is a multidimensional problem that requires, as Young *et al.* have argued, a multidimensional framework of analysis to interpret it (Young 1986). The framework should be one in which a number of relevant factors need to be considered both individually and in relation to each other if we are to reach an explanation we might want to consider comprehensive.

In their own attempt to think through what a comprehensive social explanation of crime would entail, 'Left Realists' such as Lea and Young have identified what they term 'the square of crime' as a heuristic to facilitate the task of analysis (Young 1984). Crime, they assert, is indeed a multidimensional phenomenon, and to understand it requires ex-amining four distinct though interrelated elements which constitute collectively the social relations of crime (see Diagram 6.1 below).

As Young explains:

The form (the square) consists of two dyads, a victim and an offender, and of actions and reactions: of crime and its control. This deconstruction gives us four definitional elements of crime: a victim, an offender, formal control and informal control. Realism then points to a square of crime involving the interaction between police and other agencies of social control, the public, the *offender* and the *victim*. Crime rates are generated not only by the interplay of these four factors but as *social relationships* between each point in the square. It is the relationship between the police and the public

Police   Offender

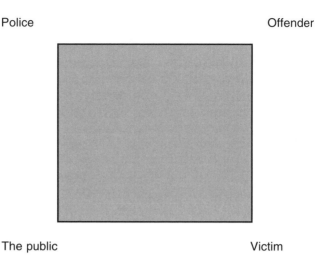

The public   Victim

Diagram 6.1   The Square of Crime

> that determines the efficacy of policing, the relationship between
> the victim and the offender which determines the impact of crime,
> and the relationship between the state and the offender which is a
> major factor in recidivism; it is the burgled public which creates the
> informal economy which sustains burglary, or the police who
> create, through illegalities, a moral climate which spurs
> delinquents into crime. (Young 1997)

Given that heuristics are supposed to facilitate the task of analysis by
rendering complex reality thinkable, it could be argued that the square of
crime is by no means a particularly self-evident or an easy heuristic to
grasp – even if I remain sympathetic to the motives that inform it. The
victim and offender dyad is clearly relevant, as is the reference to social
control mechanisms. I fail, though, to understand why the state and
society constitute an opposed dyad, not least because the term society is
itself a reification that defies easy definition. What precisely, for example,
does it mean to suggest that society demands or wants anything? And
why impose a label called the state *and* multiagency partnerships? Surely
there is just social control both in its formal (statutory) form, along with
an array of non-statutory to informal mechanisms, and these would
certainly go further than 'multiagency partnerships'. One could think
here, for example, of parenting patterns and, not least, environmental
design as both involving an element of social control that would have a

bearing on crime patterns in significant ways. Where, though, do they fit on the square? If the answer is somewhere between the state and society, then this does not suggest a particularly coherent solution.

The routine activities approach to crime developed by Cohen and Felson (1979) offers a different and altogether more comprehensible approach to examining crime, even if, as we shall see, there is a need to develop the model in ways that move beyond the (conservative and constraining) limits of routine activity theory itself. Drawing upon ecological traditions within criminology, and applied specifically to account for direct-contact predatory victimizations, Cohen and Felson argue that for a criminal event to occur there must be a convergence within time and space of three key variables – a motivated offender, a suitable target, and an absence of capable guardians. Collectively, these factors represent the key elements that must be present for any criminal act to occur:

(a) There must be a *motivated offender* available to commit an offence for a crime to occur at all.
(b) A motivated offender, though, does not engage in crime unless there are *suitable targets* available.
(c) Crime does not occur in an institutional vacuum but always in the context of a world of *capable guardians* who have chosen to define the act as a crime and who have initiated attempts to control and prevent it.

If one or more of these key ingredients are missing then, Cohen and Felson contend, a crime will occur. People, for example, may well aspire to commit criminal acts but unless they are motivated in the sense of possessing an inclination to offend and the ability to carry through their inclination, they will not perpetrate an offence. Nor will a crime event occur if targets are neither available nor suitable to victimize. If people, for example, do not carry desirable and valuable goods, they are unlikely to be robbed in the way those that do are. For the same reason, if suitable targets are not present in vicinities that motivated offenders inhabit, then again a crime is unlikely to occur. Finally, if capable guardians impose regimes of control that make a crime either highly likely to be detected or which ensure that suitable targets are heavily defended, motivated offenders are unlikely to be deterred from crime.

Assuming that criminal motivation is a given attribute of all offenders, what routine activity theorists seek to study is 'the manner in which the spatio-temporal organisation of human activities creates opportunities that help people translate criminal inclination into action' (Cohen 1980).

In effect, their hypothesis suggests that, to understand and explain crime it is necessary to examine the factors that act both to facilitate or hinder the convergence in time and space of the three components they identify as integral to the criminal act. What they choose to study in order to account for these is what they identify as routine activity. This they define as the daily activities or lifestyle in which people routinely engage and which on occasion can act to place them either at a greater or lesser risk of crime. Caywood summarizes the position aptly:

> As Cohen and Felson (1979) note, many daily activities separate people from those that they trust and the property they value. Routine activities also bring together at various times of the day or night people of different backgrounds, sometimes in the presence of facilities, tools or weapons that influence the commission or avoidance of illegal acts. Hence the timing of when one engages in work, schooling, leisure, and other routine activities may be of central importance in explaining crime rates. (Caywood 1998)

While the identification of routine activities as key variables in explaining why crime events occur remains important, it is not my intention here to look in more detail at routine activity theory *per se* or suggest that it provides or can provide a compelling account of street crime. Leaving aside a number of key weaknesses inherent in this approach (which are beyond the scope of this enquiry), what I want to focus upon is the strength of the framework that Cohen and Felson have developed to explain crime. This, I would suggest, is both plausible and constitutes a more convincing heuristic approach to street crime than the Left Realist idea of a square of crime. It works, I suggest, precisely because it is both easy to grasp (as all good heuristics must be); because it accounts for the essential three variables at play in any crime event; and, not least, because it provides the framework for a comprehensive social theory of crime. As with the idea of a square of crime, it suggests that any explanation must be able to account for all of the key variables – motivated offenders, targets and the absence of suitable guardians – and explain the interrelation between them. It avoids, however, extraneous variables such as 'society', which are not particularly helpful, as we have noted.

As opposed to a heuristic conceptualized as two dyads coming together in the form of a square composed of four elements, I will begin with the model derived from routine activity theory premised upon a triangular relation between three variables. Collectively these three variables can be reproduced in the form of a triangle such as the one represented in Diagram 6.2 below. If we use this model as the basis for explaining street crime, then the aim of a comprehensive explanation must be to account for each of these three elements and their interrelation with the other two.

Premised as it is upon a rational choice theory of human nature, routine activity theory (like control theories more generally) simply accepts that humans will, in the right circumstances, be motivated to perpetrate crime, but crucially without questioning precisely why a particular group of people as opposed to others actually become offenders. Though this *a priori* assumption about human nature does, as routine activity theories demonstrate, allow for an interesting and in some ways penetrating analysis of crime events, it is nevertheless too delimiting. If our aim is to explain street robbery in a comprehensive and fully social way, then clearly the forces that act to produce motivated offenders also need to be accommodated. To do this means shifting decisively beyond the substantive limits of routine activity theory, which simply takes motivation as given.

But this begs the question: How do we think through these causal forces and their interrelation? For the purpose of the analysis that will be subsequently developed, the question of offending will be addressed through studying the production of motivated offenders via an analysis of the array of social forces that produce them. To establish this, we need to ask why street robbers want what they seek to acquire through street robbery so much that they will break rules and engage in highly risky behaviour to get it. This invites an explanation that requires us to examine three issues.

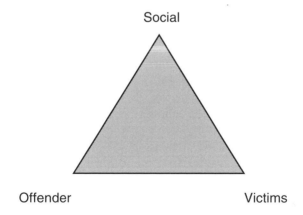

Diagram 6.2 The Aetiology of Crime

(i)   First, it is necessary to examine the nature of the aspirations and needs of street robbers as they define them. What is it they want and why do they want these particular things so urgently that they will commit crime in order to acquire them? This issue, it could be emphasized, is all about socialization. It is about the social constitution of the desires that people hold about their world and their place in it. To put this another way, if people did not possess the aspiration to accumulate the kind of thing that street robbery provides, it is unlikely that street crime would in fact occur.

(ii) Second, any attempt to explain the production of motivated offenders must then explain why these socially induced aspirations and needs cannot be satisfied through legitimate, i.e. law-abiding, means. Society after all sanctions an array of socially acceptable routes by which social aspirations can be met, and the taboos and sanctions that it imposes to ensure that people do not deviate from these are considerable.

(iii) Finally, it is necessary to examine why *only* some groups (as opposed to all) turn to street robbery in order to gratify their (frustrated) needs and desires. What factors act to ensure that the decision to perpetrate crime is in fact made? This in turn requires an investigation of the incentives both positive and negative that provoke the decision on the part of an individual or groups to perpetrate crime.

To address these issues I will deploy an approach that derives from two theoretical traditions in criminology: the *strain theory* of Robert Merton, and a *theory of differential association* derived from Edmund Sutherland. Merton's approach suggests that crime is an adaptive response to a situation where socially induced desires cannot be satisfied because the social structure of society does not universalize the means that allow this to occur (Merton 1953). In the modern state most people, whatever their social background, are socialized into a way of life that holds out certain things as desirable. In western societies, material success is one important aspect of this dominant system of values. The problem, though, is that only some groups are placed by virtue of privilege of birth in a situation that provides them with the life chances and thus the means to gratify these desires through socially legitimate avenues, i.e. getting a good job and progressing up the occupational hierarchy. Those that lack these life chances (the lower working class or minority ethnic groups) consequently experience the contradiction between what they have been taught to desire and the limited options available by which they can be gratified as a form of strain. This anomic situation may then provoke a response that may reveal itself in what Merton termed a 'deviant adaptation'. In effect, they accept the social values they have been socialized to accept, but have innovated on the social means by which these may be gratified.

It is my contention that this approach still provides the most appropriate way of addressing points (i) and (ii), precisely because it invites an examination of the sources of desire while also helping to explain precisely why these are not pursued through socially acceptable means.

Though this structural explanation provides the theoretical purchase to understand why a particular group may turn to crime as an adaptive strategy, it does not explain why only particular groups within a population that experience the same strains adapt by turning to crime while others do not. For this we need a method that facilitates an understanding of *process*. It is for this reason that an account of differential association is also required in any attempt to explain the production of motivated offenders.

For Sutherland (Sutherland 1979) people become criminal only if exposed to an excess of definitions favourable to the violation of the law over definitions unfavourable to the violation of the law. This process he defined as one of *differential association*. The capacity to commit crime is dependent upon a process of learning, which implies interactions with other people, in a process of communication. In relation to the study of street robbery, this approach is very important because it facilitates an analysis of the precise array of factors that provoke someone to embrace such crime as an adaptive strategy. What is positive about this approach is that it rests upon a conception of crime as a product of human praxis and a consequence of processes that evolve over time and in space. In recognizing these features, this framework invites a criminology which, while aware of structural determinants, avoids reification and by association an over-socialized view of the individual. It accomplishes this by locating an understanding of deviance in relation to an array of micro social processes at play between an individual and the cultural environment in which he or she is located.

If we now consider the kind of micro processes at play, a number of factors need to be considered. These include the study of the routine activities of offender populations; the relation between would-be offenders and those who already offend; the seductions and pleasures attached to participating in street crime; and a consideration of how deviant identities are consequently stabilized and reproduced. As we will have cause to note, the analysis of these areas also invites consideration of other research traditions, from labelling theory to phenomenology to subcultural theory.

In support of what might be viewed as an exercise in untoward eclecticism, this approach can be justified on the following grounds. First, a complex problem requires a complex analysis. Second, while many theories of crime are often presented as mutually antithetical to one another, this conflictual reading of theory ignores an important truth: though each theory will fail if we imagine that it can provide a comprehensive explanation of crime alone, each does touch upon and explain an important part of crime and criminal behaviour. The lesson I derive from this is that any comprehensive explanation of crime must draw upon the insights of many theories, rather than find truth in the application of one theory alone. What unifies them in the context in which I will subsequently deploy these approaches is that each contributes to the function of helping to establish the incentive structures, or as Glaster aptly describes it, the 'tipping points' that 'shift the predominant stakes of individuals from conformity to non-conformity' (Glaster, quoted in Braithwaite 1993).

For any crime to occur there must be present not only a motivated offender but, as Cohen and Felson observe, a suitable target. This term embraces people and the goods they carry, both of which can be the objects of a criminal offence. A fully social theory of street crime must explain precisely why certain groups come to be selected as suitable targets, as well as accounting for why certain populations become motivated offenders.

In their own attempt to think through the dynamics of target suitability, Felson and Cohen argue that there are four issues that require analysis (Cohen 1979). First, there are issues that pertain to the target's potential *value*. This could either be a target's material or symbolic value, each of which will affect its desirability for motivated offenders. Second, there are factors that bear on the target's *visibility*. This pertains to the potential risk of its discovery by motivated offenders. Targets that are invisible in the sense of well hidden will be less likely to be apprehended than those that are not. The third factor pertains to the target's *accessibility*. Is the target in a place or space that enables a criminal violation while also permitting the possibility of an escape? The final variable pertains to the target's *inertia*. This refers to the array of factors that make it difficult to overcome for the purpose of a criminal violation. In this sense, a product that is light, indistinguishable and easily transported will be less inert than goods that are heavy, branded and difficult to transport away and sell on.

To study street crime comprehensively it will be necessary to consider all of these factors in relation to the population of victims. We will need to explain why some groups are over-represented in the victim population, and what it is about such groups or the goods they carry that marks them out as suitable and assessable targets.

The third variable in Cohen and Felson's model pertains – as we have seen – to what they term the absence of suitable guardians. Evidently crime is perpetrated in the context of a world that has (a) defined it as such; and (b) initiated an array of efforts to prevent it. While keeping faith with the idea that guardianship is something we need to consider, my intention in what follows will be to substitute the term guardianship with the more nebulous but inclusive term 'social control'. In justification for this I would suggest that one problem that follows through from referring only to the absence of suitable guardians is that guardianship itself refers only to a limited domain of the control efforts that can have a bearing on crime. It typically signifies the presence or absence of defences, and while this is certainly a relevant consideration, it is not a sufficient one. It fails because it does not embrace the totality of controls that society imposes to prevent crime and deviance. The term, I would accept, does include ideas of situational defence and law-enforcement activity. It does not, however, include control mechanisms such as deterrent punishments, or indeed an array of proactive interventions that we might also want to consider important for preventing particular crimes. Where, for example, do social crime prevention methods such as educational programmes or rehabilitation programmes figure?

My answer to this would be to suggest that such control systems do not fall within the remit of capable guardianship. These limitations justify, therefore, the semantic shift from an analysis of guardianship to an analysis of social control, or more specifically *deficits in social control,* because that is what we need to study in order to account for street robbery. Again and self-evidently, if the array of social control systems society initiated to prevent street crime was successful, there would be no crime as it would be impossible to perpetrate.

To study the deficits in social control raises the issue of defining what social control is for the purpose of analysis. By way of a provisional definition I will define social control as the array of interventions that is imposed to prevent an offence from being committed. These include interventions that can be viewed as statutory and formal, as well as those which are non-statutory and informal. The array of interventions that fall within the remit of this definition would include responses that are reactive (that respond to an offence after it has been committed) or proactive (which are designed to prevent the likelihood of an offence being committed).

While recognizing that there are different ways to examine social control, for the purpose of this investigation I will approach its study by investigating what I will suggest constitute the four dominant approaches that we, as a western society, currently impose to prevent crime. In this respect and in this order I will examine:

- Law enforcement.
- Deterrence and punishment.
- Situational crime prevention.
- Social crime prevention.
- The integration and coordination of social control effort.

These general approaches encompass both statutory and non-statutory bodies involved either directly or indirectly in crime prevention, as well as proactive and reactive responses they may be responsible for initiating.

The term *law enforcement* includes the activities of those organizations which, like the police, have a direct role to play in preventing crime and detecting and apprehending offenders. In relation to the study of street crime, the analysis of law-enforcement activity will focus on the strategies the police deploy to prevent crime, as well as the array of practices they initiate on the basis of the strategies they follow. How, we will need to ask, do law-enforcement agencies collate the intelligence they need in order to plan their interventions? What precise tactics do they initiate to prevent robberies from occurring and what do they do to apprehend and prosecute offenders? In studying these factors we need to be aware why, either singly or in relation to each other, such initiatives fail to prevent street crime, and the reasons that may help to explain this need to be identified.

While the police are typically considered the single most important agency in the fight against crime, they are by no means the only organization whose role it is to dissuade potential criminals from engaging in criminal acts. The criminal justice system also includes an array of other organizations that play an important role in attempting to prevent crime. Important among these are those which, like the court system, exist to process and prosecute offenders, along with those parts of the penal system which exist to punish and rehabilitate them. In a society which views the successful prosecution, punishment and rehabilitation of offenders as a key element in its own war against crime, examining the impact of this institutional apparatus in relation to street crime remains very important. How successful is the prosecution service? Does prison really work to deter street criminals? And just how rehabilitated are those subjected to its administrations?

The term 'situational crime prevention' refers to what remains one of the fastest growing and, for the government and its champions, most successful crime-reduction programmes in the world. Championed by the British Home Office in the 1980s, situational crime prevention rejects the traditional focus of positivistic criminology on the study of criminal dispositions in favour of a rational choice approach that understands the criminal as a rational agent (Clarke 1980). That is, as someone who commits crime on the basis of a rational assumption that the benefits of doing so outweigh the costs. Arguing that the search for ambitious social solutions to crime is at best misguided and at worst a failed paradigm, situational crime prevention approaches issues around crime prevention in a way that seeks an effective and evidence-based approach to establishing what works and what can be done. This approach involves a process that combines the study of the opportunities that permit different crimes to occur with an analysis of the interventions that can be made to reduce them. Typically, situational crime prevention operates on the principle of seeking to manipulate the environment in ways that act to reduce the opportunity for crime and by so doing raise the social costs that would accrue from engaging in it. Or at least raising the social costs to a level that the criminal would perceive as outweighing any benefits.

Designing-out principles may be applied from redesigning material goods in order to reduce the possibility of their becoming targets for motivated offenders, through to the modification and design of entire areas. An example of the former would include the kind of design feature now regularly seen on contemporary cars such as immobilizers and alarms, both of which have had a significant effect in reducing the number of cars stolen. Examples of the latter can include the way modern estates or shopping malls are now regularly designed. This can include ensuring that the building is constructed in ways that facilitate natural surveillance, and ensuring that adequate defences, such as secure door and window locks and the installation of sophisticated surveillance systems such as CCTV, are in-built to prevent crime.

Like other crime-prevention approaches, *social crime prevention* includes interventions that are designed to reduce crime and provoke law-abiding behaviour. What distinguishes the interventions that fall within a social crime-prevention remit from the other approaches considered above is that they aspire to address the problem of crime through the promulgation of measures that are non-repressive and proactive. They are often also unified by their desire to tackle the deep causes that give rise to crime. In this sense, and unlike situational crime prevention, these kind of interventions aspire to address the motives and dispositions of offenders through seeking to modify them in ways that prevent engagement in criminal behaviour. Social approaches to crime prevention, however, can also include more ambitious social policies designed to reduce crime through re-engineering the socio-economic situation of the populations from which offenders are drawn.

Interventions that fall within the remit of social crime prevention can be include:

- Attempts to warn and inform young people about the dangers and moral consequences of rule breaking.

- The provision of activities designed to allow potential criminals to sublimate their urges in more socially benevolent ways.

- Modifying the life chances of different populations in ways that reduce the social factors that are held to constitute the structural basis of crime.

Social attempts to prevent crime can take more ostensibly criminological forms in so far as they are characterized by a conscious attempt to reduce criminal behaviour through a particular policy. They may also be non-criminological in design but nevertheless play a key crime-reduction role. Attempts to provide information to young people about crime, for example, would be an instance of the former, while using funding to regenerate high-crime run-down inner-city areas might be considered an example of the latter.

The final control strategy I will include in the study of social control responses I will generically term the coordination and integration of community safety effort. This I consider a social control strategy because at the present it is viewed as such by the government, which has devoted considerable effort and resources to develop it (Home Office 2003). In a world where crime is now supposed to be confronted by 'joined-up thinking' based on 'evidence-based policy', and where promulgating holistic solutions is the desired objective, it is clearly important to see how much of this was around as street robbery soared. Just how far were these principles consistent with practice on the ground?

In considering the *integration* of community safety effort, it will be necessary to examine whether community safety and crime reduction effort in relation to street crime are appropriately located within each of the categories of crime prevention discussed above. Are resources adequately allocated or are we as a society locating effort disproportionately in some areas of intervention at the expense of others? Another issue relevant to matters of integration is whether effort is located in ways that demonstrate an adequate balance between reactive approaches to the problem and more proactive ones. Are resources being channelled in ways that typically address the problem only by looking at the symptoms of its expression (a street crime epidemic), or are adequate steps also being taken to resource the interventions that might have a bearing on addressing its causes?

In today's mixed economy of crime prevention and community safety effort, the issue of how the various players within any locality are brought together in ways that ensure a coordinated effort also needs to be considered. How, we will need to enquire, are the diverse partners in crime control (such as the police, youth workers and probation officers) brought together in ways that ensure each organisation performs its function to promote a holistic solution to the problem? In considering this issue, it will be necessary to examine the kinds of strategic thinking that different crime-prevention partnerships engage in. Are the right players making the right decisions, and do all the players that need to be involved actually involve themselves in community safety effort? Finally, in a world governed by a managerialist culture characterized by the production of strategic plans, and where progress is charted in relation to specified benchmarks, how relevant has this culture been to ensuring that street crime has been confronted effectively?

By examining the forces that produce motivated offenders, suitable victims and deficits in social control, it is possible, I would suggest, to provide a comprehensive explanation of street crime and its contemporary rise in British society. This will also prove to be one that can explain the observable trends in street crime identified in Chapter 3.

To apply this framework of analysis, my aim will be to study each of the three strands discussed above in turn, drawing attention to the relationships between each of the constituent variables. I will begin in Chapter 7 by examining the forces that act to produce suitable victims. This will then be followed by chapters dealing respectively with the production of motivated offenders, and the consideration of deficits in the social control response.

Street crime, as we saw in the previous chapter, occurs at different rates in different times and places. While the task of explaining it must draw attention to factors that are common to all street crime, analysis must also be susceptible to a range of variant factors that explain why street crime rates not only change over time but in relation to place. In order to accomplish this task, my aim will be to draw where appropriate upon recent and relevant research conducted by others. I will also, however, draw directly upon the research I conducted in Lambeth between 2001 and 2002 on rising street robbery in the area.

As a research laboratory for studying street robbery, Lambeth is quite unique. For those unfamiliar with the area, it is a multiply deprived borough located in southeast London, which in recent years has achieved the unenviable reputation of having the highest rate of street crime in London, and one of the highest rates in the UK. The research was undertaken in 2002, at the height of what would become an intense moral panic around the issue. The research was funded by Government Office for London and involved a number of research methods. These included conducting interviews with young offenders, community safety practitioners, police officers and the heads of local statutory services. The research also involved an analysis of available police data on street crime, and drew upon a range of socio-economic and demographic data produced by the local authority. By using Lambeth as a case study, I believe it is possible to examine the problem of street robbery in contemporary society. In the chapters that follow, the results of this research will be referred to on a regular basis.

Part 3
Street Robbery and
Contemporary Society

Chapter 7

Suitable and available victims

Just as bakers need grain and construction workers bricks, so street robbers require victims to rob. To understand the phenomenon of street crime, it is therefore important to study a range of interrelated factors connected with becoming both a suitable and available victim for a street robbery. First, we need to establish why more people appear in recent years more suitable as victims than was previously the case. Second, we need to understand the factors that leave more people vulnerable to attack than previously. Finally, we need to examine these factors in relation to the availability of victims to motivated offenders.

To begin with, I will argue that more people are more likely to possess the objects coveted by street robbers than was hitherto the case, a factor which has dramatically increased the population of potential targets for street robbery. I will then argue that not only are there more potential targets, but that the desirable goods possessed by potential victims are relatively *assessable*, often *visible* and are characterized by low rates of *inertia*, all of which raise the likelihood of victimization. This, I will argue, has occurred at the same time as the possibility of access to victims of other categories of crime has actually decreased. Finally, I will suggest that increasing target suitability is also accompanied by a net increase in patterns of victim accessibility to motivated offenders.

Young people, who are the fastest-growing population of street robbery victims, are not only more likely to carry the goods coveted by street robbers, but they are also typically located in spatially compressed areas that leave them inherently vulnerable to victimization by motivated offenders they find difficulty in avoiding. New patterns in economic development, however, also create the preconditions necessary for rising patterns of victimization by attracting suitable victims into areas where motivated offenders are likely to dwell. This factor, I will suggest, can explain why areas such as Lambeth have disproportionately higher levels of street robbery than other areas. I will consider each of these arguments in turn.

For a population to find themselves a target they must possess at the least an array of desirable goods that distinguish them as suitable victims. They must possess items that are not only coveted and consequently desired by motivated offenders, but coveted and desired to the extent that offenders will break the law and risk serious punishment in order to obtain them.

As we saw in Chapter 3, the kind of goods desired by street robbers include cash, jewellery and, increasingly, mobile phones. Indeed, as Home Office figures attest, mobile phone theft remains one of the striking features of the recent surge in street robbery more generally. Recorded mobile phone thefts, these figures show, have at least doubled between 1998 and 2001, while the growth in phone robberies over the last three years that involve only a phone, as opposed to a phone and other goods, have also increased dramatically (Harrington 2001). In 2001, 330,000 offences involving mobile phones were recorded by the police, constituting 6 per cent of all recorded crime. Indeed, if mobile phone theft perpetrated specifically by young people were taken out of the figures for street robbery, then the surge in street crime in recent years would not have occasioned the surprise it subsequently generated.

While affluent populations have always carried goods such as money, jewellery and credit cards, the development of mobile phone technology and its associated market penetration have created a situation where such goods are also routinely and regularly carried by large numbers of the population. Not only, therefore, is it the case that the wider population carries the very things that street robbers covet, but it is also the case that more people than ever before are now carrying these objects.

As the statistics testify, the growth in mobile phone possession in the last ten years has been phenomenal. As Table 7.1, taken from a Mori Tracker Survey, indicates, whereas in January 2000 46 per cent of adults living in the UK possessed a mobile phone, by February 2002 that figure had risen to 73 per cent, a rise of more than 50 per cent in a period of only 25 months (Oftel 2003). Figures produced by Mori also indicate that growth is greatest among the population most likely to figure as a victim of street robbery, i.e. the 15–35 age group. Within this age category, over 80 per cent of the population is an owner or possessor of a mobile phone (Oftel 2002). Mobile phone use by younger people has also been the fastest-growing sector of the market. As we saw earlier, this population also figures as the largest and fastest-growing population for street robberies in general and mobile phone thefts in particular. Cumulatively, the consequences of such growth have been to ensure that the potential number of victims has increased significantly. This helps to answer the question, 'Why is street crime rising more generally across the UK?' The answer to this is that more people are now carrying the disposable goods street criminals have been taught to covet and desire.

The suitability of these consumer goods as objects of desire on the part of street robbers has increased not only because these goods possess a symbolic and material value to motivated offenders, but because they are also very vulnerable to attack. They are certainly more vulnerable to attack than acquiring desirable goods through perpetrating other kinds of acquisitive crime such as burglary.

In a street robbery event, the victim is typically confronted with overwhelming force. This is used specifically to appropriate goods that are typically small and which are relatively easily obtained from the victim, either through a snatch, through violence or by the threat of violence. Though, as we will see in more detail in the next chapter, the act of street robbery does take some courage to perpetrate and some skill to perpetrate well, it is an event that is relatively easy to learn, particularly if the teachers are able and the potential offender is fit and fleet of foot.

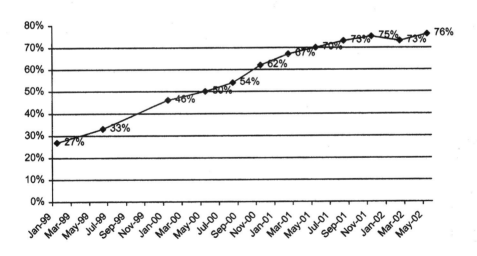

Table 7.1:   Mobile growth – % UK adults who have/use a mobile phone
Source: Oftel 2002.

As a street robbery typically takes a very small amount of time to perpetrate and remains relatively invisible to other users of public space, despite its public nature, it is unlikely to set in motion an event that will easily attract wider attention and intervention. Even if it is witnessed, as in the case of a snatch, it might well be too late to intervene because the perpetrator has already made good his escape. If a blitz-style assault is used, what psychologists term 'the bystander effect' will often take over. This refers to a general unwillingness to intervene when faced with problematic situations that do not involve the person concerned. Given that a witness is often likely to be physically weaker than an assailant, or is confronted by a number of assailants, standing by could well be read as an exercise in pragmatic self-preservation. It does not necessarily mean indifference to the plight of a victim. Given that victims of street crime are also unlikely to carry weapons themselves, and are chosen precisely because of their vulnerability anyway, this also makes them eminently suitable as potential targets. Street robbery, then, remains a popular crime not only because people carry what street robbers desire, but also because these goods can be fairly easily removed from victims, who anyway are selected because they are vulnerable.

The attractiveness of the goods desired by street robbers is contingent not only on its direct monetary or symbolic value, but also on whether or not such goods can be distributed with relative ease to illegal grey markets where they are exchanged for hard currency or reused. Money, of course, is the most useful of the goods appropriated through street robbery, as it can be used directly by the robbers involved. This is why many robbers prefer money. Other goods acquired through street robbery require more effort to valorize, as they must be disposed of through more complex channels. That noted, it is also evident that there is a ready market for goods such as jewellery, cameras and laptop computers, as the street robbers I interviewed confirmed. At its most disorganized and informal, the illegal market into which stolen goods could be distributed includes friends and acquaintances. At its most organized it could involve well-organized criminal fraternities. These networks operate both by providing motivated offenders with specific requests for particular items (this style of phone with this specification), while also supplying the robber with access to those who would undertake to sell the stolen goods on.

Mobile phones clearly play a prominent role in this illegal economy, not only because there are lots of people who would be prepared to steal them, but also because many others would be prepared to purchase stolen ones. They could also, at least until recently, be manipulated in ways that allowed them to be reused once stolen, not least by having their sim cards replaced. The failure of mobile phone producers to immobilize stolen phones, and the subsequent failure of the government to compel the producers to do so, also enhanced the relative value of mobile phones as objects of choice on the black economy, a point to which I will return. Cumulatively, the irresponsibility attached to this failure to act has helped to fan the flames of the subsequent crime harvest. As young men testified, in a demand-led economy there was a ready market for the goods that street crime delivered.

The likelihood of becoming a victim, as we saw above, is contingent upon factors that relate not only to the goods that victims carry, but also to factors specific and peculiar to the targeted individual. As young men involved in street robbery explained, there are factors specific to victims they would take cognisance of prior to planning an attack. First, they would select a place where they thought suitable victims would congregate. Second, they would plan potential escape routes. Third, they would, where possible, ensure that those they did target were relatively vulnerable. For this reason women were often selected. Men would be as well, but when this occurred it often involved a number of perpetrators. In the case of young people, the pattern of victimization was always characterized by a noticeable power relation. The strong attack the weak, the older the younger, many against one, and so on. The decision to target a specific individual was also determined by the things they would do. Talking on a mobile phone ensured that a potential victim would be distracted and therefore unaware they were being targeted. Such behaviour also signified to the street robber that this was a person worth targeting, while the obvious visibility of the object made it easy to appropriate, specifically in the context of a snatch.

Perpetrators also demonstrated a sharp awareness of the routine activities of victims. They would know, for example, when specific individuals would congregate in areas amenable to robbery. The more professional among them would also know the time and days when they would have been paid. The kinds of streetwise knowledge perpetrators were able to demonstrate also extended to an understanding of routine behaviours victims might engage in at specific places. They would know that businessmen often stop outside tube stations to check for messages on their mobile phones. Street crime, it could be observed, is an act by no means perpetrated by mindless or stupid people. Like many things in life, it requires considerable skill to do well.

Law-enforcement activity was also something that street robbers would consider in selecting areas to target. This would go hand in hand with an understanding of the locations of CCTV emplacements and areas that should be avoided. This streetwise knowledge is best demonstrated by the effect of law-enforcement activity upon street crime in a given area. As the police continually report, efforts to 'crack down' on a particular hot spot invariably displace the problem elsewhere. In the face of the safer streets campaign launched by the Metropolitan Police against street robbery in 2002, one of the young men claimed that 'no one robs in Brixton anymore' because 'there are too many police vans driving up and down', and went on to describe how he and his friends would target other less visibly defended areas, particularly those where 'large numbers of people gather and which are dark'. Gains made in one place by community safety effort were simply offset by increases in other areas as the street robbers moved on. In a street culture where 'getting one over' on the 'feds' and avoiding the 'bully-vans' are established rules in the game of street crime, knowing how to avoid law enforcement was a skill young men came to acquire early in their criminal careers.

Victim selection, on the other hand, was heightened by the ignorance of victims *vis-à-vis* their potential vulnerability. Walking around areas such as Brixton carrying handbags that could easily be snatched (in ways that wearing a small rucksack cannot), or wearing a suit and standing outside a tube station talking on an expensive mobile phone, self-evidently enhance potential victim status. These, after all, are precisely the signs street robbers look out for. In other words, victims can present themselves in ways that raise the possibility of their victimization.

Victim availability, however, is also shaped by the behaviours that victims routinely engage in, for their routine behaviour also creates the conditions that act to bring them into contact with motivated offenders. To understand rising street robbery, we need to look at these routine behaviours in the ways suggested by routine activity theory and account for the factors that explain them. As we do this, we also need to be aware of changing patterns of routine behaviour over time, because in some cases this can also help to explain growing patterns of street crime in high-crime areas.

Rather than address these issues by examining routine behaviour in relation to the victim population in general, we need to divide the victim population into two distinct groups for the purpose of analysis. We need to do this because the victimization of the young and older age groups is rather different. In what follows, therefore, I will consider the routine behaviour of young people then the population of adult victims.

Street crime, by its name and by its nature, is an offence perpetrated in the context of public space. As we saw in Chapter 3, this could mean playgrounds, streets, pathways and parks (Smith 2003). To understand why young people are so disproportionately over-represented as victims of street robbery, we need to study the factors that bring them onto the street where they can become victims. We also need to study this in relation to the factors that have led to street crime being recorded as one of the principal means by which young people now regularly victimize each other. This is not an unimportant or trivial factor, for this can also help to explain the dramatic surge in street crime we have witnessed in recent years.

Young people in general, and young men in particular, typically spend their day-to-day leisure lives in the context of the street. The street provides young people not only with a place to meet and socialize, but also with an opportunity to plan and execute different activities. It is in the street, for example, that they commune as friends; it is on the streets that they make their way to and from school; and it is in the context of street life that they engage in or find themselves the victims of street crime.

While adults often find the presence of young people gathering together on the streets threatening, it could also be pointed out that street life is by its nature exciting. It always has been. This is where thrills are to be found and where the identity of young people is also forged. There are, however, a range of other factors that act independently of the enjoyment factor to propel young people onto the street and into the vicinity of those who would perpetrate street robbery.

In run-down inner-city areas the presence of young people on the street is also conditioned by other factors that pertain to the socio-economics of the area. The first factor that may be identified pertains to the paucity of services and facilities available to young people. In the case of Lambeth, for example, the services available to young people have been decimated in recent decades by regular and sustained cuts to youth services. While youth services can and are offered through the mechanism of the free market, much of what is on offer in Lambeth is often too expensive for young people on poor estates to use. In my investigation into the roots of street crime in Lambeth I discovered that some areas of the borough were devoid of youth services altogether. These factors, acting in conjunction with poor and often overcrowded housing, help to propel young people onto the street because in effect there is no alternative available to them. Being spatially compressed not only in high-density estates, but also in other high-density environments in which the adult world chooses to corral them, clearly raises the probability of victimization. Such routine activity invariably raises the likelihood of becoming a victim of street crime, precisely because these activities place young people in a risk environment where dangers of many kinds await them.

Street life, while exciting, can also be dangerous. Unsurprisingly, it is in the context of street life that young people can find themselves victimized in many ways. This can include being bullied by an individual or gang, or being harassed on the way to or from school. While fights can be viewed as 'fun' by young people, they can also be dangerous, particularly when weapons are used. Fear of being victimized can also lead to adaptive behaviours such as self-imposed curfews or avoiding specific places at particular times. In high-density areas such as local council estates, where young people live in a situation characterized by a high degree of spatial compression, avoiding such conflict is difficult. Sheer availability entails a high possibility of victimization, and increasingly the form in which victimization is expressed is what is regarded as street robbery.

The motives that justify victimization may appear from the outside relatively trivial. It could be because you are in the wrong place at the wrong time, or because you have intruded into space 'owned' by another group of young people who claim proprietorial rights to it. Disputes could also arise because somebody may have slighted someone else's honour, which requires a demonstration of physical force in order to restore respect in a world where respect is everything. Where, until recently, such disputes would routinely have been dealt with by reference to traditional means including threats, intimidation and violence, what we are now witnessing, I will suggest, is a significant change in the form of such proceedings. In addition to these existing modes of street-level conflict, what we are now witnessing are violent moves to separate victims from the desirable material objects they increasingly possess, specifically mobile phones. While the growth in mobile phone ownership among young people is a factor fuelling this, it must be noted that this is *not* impacting on the incidence or prevalence of victimization. It is more likely, I would suggest, that existing patterns of victimization are now regularly perpetrated through alternative means. In other words, if you bully someone you rob them. If you want to humiliate an enemy you rob them. If you want to demonstrate control of an area you rob someone. Robbery in effect represents a new means by which older forms of youth conflict are now regularly fought out. It becomes an important measure by which the power relations of the street are routinely established and reproduced in many areas of our cities. Robbery then, while a mechanism for acquiring desirable goods, is also a means by which a power relation is demonstrated. It could in this sense justifiably be viewed as a way of symbolically emasculating someone.

Because existing patterns of street conflict among young people are now increasingly attached to an act of robbery, in effect a new offence has been created. This is what is coded within the official statistics as street crime. Until recently, most of these low-intensity conflicts would have gone largely unreported, either because nothing was stolen or because these traditional forms of conflict do not tend to occasion too much adult investigation. After all, traditionally, this is what the adult world presupposes young men do. Because an object of value (a phone) is now routinely stolen, the report rate will consequently tend to be far higher. The reason for this is simple: in order to get a replacement phone, a crime number is required by the insurance companies concerned. Rising levels of street crime among young people can therefore be explained in terms that need not presuppose a world of greater victimization by an ever more predatory population of offenders, or because there are more perpetrators on the streets. The increase occurs because a growing number of these conflicts now involve robbery and are reported and recorded as such.

In the case of young people who are victims, it would appear that a number of factors could lead to their victimization, independent of the fact that they routinely carry the kinds of goods motivated offenders would covet. Being in the wrong place at the wrong time could certainly be regarded as a high-risk factor. In particular, from young offenders' testimony it would appear that straying onto someone else's 'manor' or turf could automatically lead someone to being selected for a 'jacking' or indeed a stabbing. In response to such a transgression, a 'fine' was imposed in the form of the disposable goods the young person carried.

Social presentation of self could also be important. 'Holding yourself timid', as one young man explained, suggested that someone would be relatively easy to target. It signified physical and, not least, mental vulnerability. Dressing in inappropriate brand labels or, worse still, in non-branded clothes, could also mark out a young person as a suitable victim. 'Low brands', as young people term them (by which they meant brands such as High Tech), suggest to would-be robbers that someone is in effect a non-person. For in the hyper-real world of postmodern consumer culture, what this act of sartorial deviance is read to intimate is that the person is someone to whom no respect is due. As one young man explained:

> If you had someone who look like a tramp come up and try and talk to you are you really going to want to speak? But if you is dressed nice, and have good things, you going to take them serious.

Inappropriate consumption could single out someone who deserved to be victimized. In effect, by not according to the demand of being appropriately attired as coded by young people (who were as much motivated offenders as consumers), a person brings victimization upon themself. To put this another way, by virtue of brand ignorance they could be 'jacked'.

A young street robber explained this to me in graphic terms as we stood one afternoon on a street corner: 'See that kid, he's crying out for it. He's asking to be jacked.' The kid in question was young, and was dressed in clothes that did not approximate in shape or form to the gangster fashion the young man I was interviewing was wearing. He stood nervously on the street, clearly unaware of 'holding himself timid', as my interviewee summarized. Again, another risk factor that marked him out as a suitable victim. As the street robber also explained, it wasn't just people like this who would find themselves targeted for a 'jacking'. Victimization could also be attributed to the fact that someone had no friends, either because they lacked appropriate social skills or were new to an estate or area. In either case, they were not a somebody – a person to whom respect could be accorded. This defined those whose failure to have and wear the right things in the right way marked them out as suitable victims.

Unsurprisingly, young people, not being stupid and being all too aware of the risks posed by demonstrating inappropriate consumption habits, often adopted an adaptive strategy of appropriate consumption in order to minimize the risks they could expect in street life. Typically, in order to avoid victimization, they would become – as far as possible – mirror images of the very people who victimized them. In effect, they looked the look, walked the walk and talked the talk of the urban street gangster. In street parlance, they 'thugged-up'. They tried to look and act hard, and by so doing demonstrated in their social presentation of self that they not suitable victims. In some cases, as we shall observe in the chapter on offenders, victim avoidance could also include becoming a street robber.

By no means unrelated to this, the possibility of becoming a victim could also be related to moves on the part of local toughs to impose their own level of street discipline, in particular over other groups of young people who conformed to a different array of subcultural values. In an interview conducted with young women in Brighton, they explained how street robbery had recently entered their life. Where once they would sit peacefully among their friends in a local park in the centre of Brighton, they now found this increasingly difficult to do. The danger they faced emanated from a group they identified as the 'townies', violent young men dressed in designer track suits who would routinely attack and rob them. Their motive would appear to be both a love of violence and their hatred of a group which had consciously adopted a more visible counter-culture style (they did not wear designer clothes and favoured instead a second-hand, more ostensibly grungy look). Though mobile phones could be and were stolen, the act of robbery often involved taking marijuana from these young bohemians. An offence, needless to say, which also meant that it could not and would not be reported to law-enforcement agencies.

If these factors help explain why younger populations are victimised, they do not explain patterns of street robbery directed at older age groups. To study patterns of victimization among this population – particularly in areas such as Lambeth, where a higher than average proportion of the victim population are in the over-18 age group – we need once again to study the changing routine activities of this population. In particular, we need to study how such routine behaviours have changed in relation to changes in the demography and socio-economic profile of the area. These, as we shall observe, have also acted to widen the potential pool of victims in an area where there are many motivated offenders.

Following the urban disorders of the late 1970s, Lambeth underwent a significant process of urban regeneration designed to alleviate its status as one of London's poorest and most multiply deprived boroughs. This has involved a significant investment in projects designed to improve the physical environment of the borough and to help and support local businesses and retailers. If we examine how regeneration has impacted on life in Lambeth, three specific developments may be observed, all of which have implications for patterns of victimization in the area.

The first way in which the impact of urban regeneration may be observed is via the process of 'gentrification' occasioned by the movement of affluent and predominantly white populations into Lambeth. This process of reverse colonization is common to other poor London boroughs, and a principal motive driving it forward appears to be access to private housing stock that is relatively more affordable than property in more affluent boroughs. An economic regeneration strategy implemented by the council designed to improve the physical environment of the borough may also be important in stimulating this demographic shift. This involved an attempt to make Lambeth more public-friendly by renovating its decaying parks and public spaces, particularly those on major arterial routes leading through the borough.[1]

Apart from the renovation of the physical environment, a considerable slice of the regeneration pie was also invested in Lambeth's economic base. The relative success of this initiative is evident in two key developments: firstly, by the redevelopment of Brixton as a thriving shopping complex, and secondly, by the sustained growth within Brixton of a highly developed night-time economy (Hobbs 2002). The first of these developments is evident in the reconstruction of Brixton centre as a thriving retail centre that provides a large surrounding population with access to a wide array of desirable consumer goods. While attempts to stimulate the local economy through support for local businesses and the use of money to improve the physical landscape remain important determinants in the regeneration process, this has also been fuelled by the movement of new people into the borough with disposable incomes to spend.

The development of the night-time economy can be related to the associated renaissance of Brixton as a cultural centre. This development is evident particularly in an array of popular new clubs, bars and restaurants in the area. Drawing specifically on Brixton's rich cultural history and not least the cachet associated with its notoriety, this development has attracted a significant transitory population. Given the late opening hours of this cultural complex in a 24 hour city culture, this development acts as a magnet to a large transitory, predominantly white and affluent population over a prolonged period of time.

The movement of this population is also facilitated by Brixton's proximity to central London, and the importance of the Victoria Line and the vicinity of Lambeth to the Northern Line cannot be underestimated. Its location in relation to major arterial roads may also be considered in this respect.

Cumulatively, as an unintended consequence of these patterns of regeneration, the social demographics of Lambeth in general and Brixton in particular have altered significantly in the last 20 years. More specifically, the consequence of these processes has been to bring new affluent adult populations into the area, and it is these populations that constitute a significant proportion of the victim population. One answer, therefore, to the question 'Why is street crime rising so fast in Lambeth?' is that there are more available targets by virtue of its regeneration.

There are a number of reasons why this population of victims can be considered suitable targets for street robbers. First, this is a population which is predominantly affluent and whose routine activities place it in close proximity to potential offenders living on the local estates. It either lives locally, shops locally or travels to the area to pursue a range of diverse leisure activities. Though, as we shall see in the next chapter, socio-economic disadvantage is also a key to explaining rising street robbery in deprived areas like Lambeth, an important point to bear in mind is that regeneration is a major driver behind rising street robbery.

In conclusion, this chapter has looked at an array of factors that together act to produce suitable and available victims for street robbers to target. The chapter has shown how over recent years more people than ever before are now carrying the material goods increasingly desired and coveted by street robbers. The chapter also explored how the value of these goods to street robbers is related both to their material value and to the ease with which they can be appropriated from victims and disposed of afterwards. The production of victims, as this chapter made clear, is also contingent upon the way victims look and behave and present themselves to the world. Finally, the chapter examined the social factors that can, as the case of Lambeth illustrates, produce the preconditions where street crime can rise by making more suitable victims available to motivated offenders. In the chapter that follows, we will turn our attention away from the situation of the victim to examine the factors that act to produce motivated offenders.

Note

1   I was a recipient of this renovation while living in Lambeth during the 1980s. As a local resident I found that our front gardens had been deemed in need of renovation and that a considerable slice of public money was to be spent on renovating and rebuilding them. As a student I was of course delighted if somewhat disturbed by such largesse being extended to an area that was by no means impoverished.

Chapter 8

The production of motivated offenders

In examining how and why young people become involved in street robbery, a number of issues need to be addressed. First, we need to establish where the will to consume the objects street robbers wish to appropriate through robbery comes from. Second, we need to consider why they appropriate these objects of desire through the medium of street robbery, as opposed to appropriating desirable goods through more legitimate avenues. Third, we must then explain why only some young people come to engage in street robbery as the chosen strategy of appropriation. This, as we shall see, will mean examining the characteristics of the outlaw cultures where street crime is practised and, not least, attending to the seductions and pleasures attendant on the act of street robbery itself.

To investigate the reasons that impel young people, and in particular young men, to engage in street crime we must as a precursor understand the reasons that lead them to engage initially in offending behaviour. To do this we must understand why they wish to acquire the kinds of goods suitable victims regularly carry, and explore why they seek to acquire these objects through the medium of offences such as street crime. To examine this, we must begin by looking not at issues of faulty socialization (the focus of underclass thinking, as we saw in Chapter 4) but at the forms of *successful socialization* young people are subjected to in free-market societies.

To interpret this we must examine why young people who engage in street robbery desire so intensely the commodities street crime provides illegal access to. Why, we must ask, do they come to covet these objects of desire so intensely that some will embark upon illegal acts in order to possess them? While one answer to this question might be to suggest that such desires represent aberrant personality traits on the part of those who hold them, this, I suggest, is the wrong way of looking at the issue. A more productive line of enquiry involves seeing such desires not as deviant but as a common trait evident in most young people. More to the point, it is my contention that if we want to understand from where the will to possess desirable objects derives, then its proximate cause is exposure to and socialization into capitalist consumption norms stimulated by capitalist culture industries.

Let us consider this in more detail. What I am proposing is that young offenders are products of a society in which the consumption of material goods is an integral aspect of their lives. As such, it is a universally distributed desire. It is something acquired, moreover, via a range of sources. It is a message they see mediated through the medium of advertising which targets them directly; it is something they learn to acquire through direct involvement in consumption rituals, either as observers or as active consumers themselves. As we shall now see, the impact of being produced as consuming beings in free-market societies has important implications for how young people live and perceive the world around them.

In their exposure to the consumer society, young people learn from a very early age that wellbeing and success in life are contingent upon the possession of desirable goods. In particular, branded goods marketed to them by the culture industries. They are also taught, and from a very early age are given to understand, that through the possession of these desirable objects – the right trousers, trainers and accessories such as mobile phones – other desirable things follow, including self-respect and the respect of others. In and through mass consumption, identities are produced and reproduced. In consumption, a lifestyle is simultaneously lived and constructed. To 'be' is literally to be in a world defined by the possession of these desirable goods. Possession defines the bearer, not only as a possessor of what everyone desires, but as a viable and sovereign agent in his or her own right.

In the possession of desired goods, things are not simply appropriated – identities are also produced and reproduced. By and through processes of cultural appropriation, a sense of who and what you are is constructed while, in the competitive order of the young, a sense of distinction relative to other people is forged. The consequences of this process are stark. Your status relative to others is marked out and defined by the kind of phone you possess, the trousers you wear, and the way you wear them. Possession of desired goods also provides a visible marker that defines where you stand relative to others in the world around you. Non-possession conversely entails an absence of these values. It is a world of non-being, of not being part of the in-group. You stand by virtue of non-consumption or ineffective consumption as a non-person, someone to whom respect is not conceded in a world in which respect is everything. In the words of one young man, it meant 'not being on the level'. As he then put it, 'You're like a no one.' This, translated literally, meant being outside the circle of being and belonging. It rendered you someone to whom no status in the world could be conceded; it could define you – as we saw in the last chapter – as a victim.

The culture industries consciously accentuate these trends through the way they brand and market their goods. Maintaining high prices stimulates the market for exclusive goods that confer high status among young people. At the same time, the corporations, by drawing heavily and parasitically on street culture (the hip-hop gangster look, for example) reproduce it in a commodified form. This is then sold back as a lifestyle option other young people are invited to emulate. The rise and fall of various consumer fads, the advent of new technologies and the constant succession of new models accentuate these trends further. Excessive profiteering by the corporations promoting desirable branded goods also exacerbates the problem because it makes the brands that are most desired impossible to obtain within the financial constraints poor populations face. The in-built obsolescence of desirable consumer goods also feeds this problem because it forges an incessant desire among young people for next years' model, which means socially generated needs can never be finally realized anyway. In effect, the consumer society produces a world of always unrealized and ultimately unrealizable desires. The trousers you are obligated to want this year are obsolete in fashion terms by the next, while this mobile phone will be replaced by the next model, and so on. At the dark heart of this consumption revolution can be found a process with sinister implications: As Cote and Allahar aptly describe it, 'What lies at the heart of this activity, however, is the fact that the media can sell young people some element of an identity they have been taught to crave' (Cote and Allahar 1996).

Though the transformation of young people into effective consumers has always been important to capitalist societies – at least since young people were first identified as conspicuous consumers in the postwar period (Miles 2000) – the nature of youth consumption has changed significantly in recent decades. From an exercise directed at purchasing the good life in the context of rising affluence under conditions of postwar welfare state capitalism it had become by the 1990s a rite of passage into everyday 'normal' life in a free-market, neo-liberal society.

As Miles explains: 'By the 1980s it was almost as if consumerism had emerged as a way of life for young people. Not only did it represent a valuable means of self-expression, but it provided a resource for the construction of their everyday life' (Miles 2000). What he means by this is that they represent the vanguard of a social movement that has witnessed not only the decline of a society in which identities were constructed through solidarity with other peer groups (such as your class of origin), but the advent of an era in which identity is now forged in and through consumption alone.

Not only has the social meaning of consumption changed for young people, but it has also changed in relation to the growing intensity of their exposure to it. They are now not only engaged in the rites of consumption from an early age, but are also subject to an advertising industry that ruthlessly targets them in ever more sophisticated ways (Klein 2001). At the heart of the crime problem as it unfolds across the UK, we consequently find an extreme form of commodity fetishism at play. My thesis is that this particular form of fetishism brings with it the desires that stimulate the insatiable demand for objects that are subsequently apprehended in the act of street robbery.

While the will to consume is a universal disposition into which all young people are socialized, the free-market society is not an economic order that universalizes the means necessary to ensure that all young people can appropriate the social goods that they have been taught to desire legitimately. In a free-market capitalist society that both produces and tolerates wide and growing inequalities, what we find is a socio-economic reality in which certain populations are accorded the means to gratify their consumption desires, while others are located in socio-economic conditions that effectively prohibit consumption. What distinguishes these two populations is their differential access to life chances. These include labour market opportunities and established wealth that allows consumption desires to be socially realized in legitimate ways.

The differential distribution of life chances can be starkly observed if we consider once again the case of Lambeth, and the socio-economic characteristics of the area. While the borough is home, as we have seen, to a predominantly white affluent population, well-equipped with the resources that will allow it to consume easily and legitimately, the same cannot be said for more deprived communities, including Lambeth's black population, which also produce the majority of its offenders. For while Lambeth has witnessed a significant process of economic and social regeneration over the last two decades, the effects of regeneration have been very uneven and not everyone can be considered winners in the process. The socio-economic position of young working-class people – particularly young black people on the estates – remains desperately poor, as deprivation indicators for the area testify. Unemployment, for example, remains at around 40 per cent on the estates in the area. This is far higher than the average unemployment rates for London and the UK as a whole. To this must be added a range of factors which enhance deprivation and social exclusion more generally. These would include the impact of institutional and overt discrimination towards the black community, particularly young black males, that limits entry into the labour market. One young man explained graphically why robbery became for him and his friends a career choice:

> Some of them do it, yes, for the money, but most of them can't get money from their parents most times. And then most don't work. And some of my friends don't have homes so they have to be hustling. They have to make money somehow.

Benefits for poorer populations are also harder to obtain, given the governmental response to what has been represented as a 'culture of dependency'. For the same reasons, young people under 18 are now unable to claim any benefits at all. If we consider the impact of receiving low rates of benefit in conjunction with living in the most expensive city in the UK, it is evident that poor populations in Lambeth find it extraordinarily hard to sustain a minimal lifestyle, let alone gratify overt consumption desires they have been taught to regard as normal. As one young man expressed this:

> I don't want to blame it all on Britain … but living in Brixton is hard.

Significant patterns of change in the postwar economy have also reinforced the entrenched deprivation. In particular, the decline of the manufacturing sector in the last three decades has had the effect of removing labour market opportunities from many working-class areas. This has two knock-on effects: first, it acts to sustain mass unemployment among young people and thus their exclusion from participating in legitimate consumption; and second, exclusion from the labour market prolongs the state of adolescence and disrupts an orderly transition into adulthood on the part of young people in this situation. It does this by removing from them the rituals, interdependencies and security that secure jobs once provided, and which in their possession would once have confirmed an adult identity. One consequence of these changes has been to compress young men together for large parts of their day-to-day lives on local streets. Another, as noted by Rutherford, has been to increase pressure on already highly pressurized families, many of whom are also welfare-dependent (Rutherford 1997). This in turn produces a pattern of routine activity that creates the space in which street robbery becomes a distinct possibility. To escape from over-crowded and often highly pressurized family units, young men congregate in the streets. There, the conditions are created both for meeting and having to deal with outlaw cultures that practise street robbery, while also placing young men in proximity to populations of assessable and suitable victims. In other words, into conjunction with more affluent populations who, as we have seen, carry the very goods poorer sections of the community cannot readily appropriate legitimately. Economic change, then, itself helps to sustain an environment that is highly conducive to crime.

The situation in poor inner-city areas like Lambeth is consequently characterized by patterns of real deprivation and poverty among certain sections of its population. Like the affluent society around them, however, these populations also share the dream of a good life defined in material terms. This is thus a population characterized not only by real deprivation, but also by intensifying levels of relative deprivation as well. Together, these factors have created what criminologists such as Lea and Young (Young 1984) would consider to be a highly criminogenic environment. In effect, it is my premise that by failing to universalize the conditions by which desirable goods may be universally appropriated, the free-market society has created a situation in which some young people have 'innovated' in their consumption. They do so by becoming involved in cultures that sanction rule-breaking. Unable to consume legitimately, many have come to develop innovative consumption strategies, one of which is street crime.

The turn towards street crime can therefore be viewed as a practical and rational resolution of the contradiction of being socialized into a world which shapes you to aspire to the consistent consumption of material goods and being located in a socio-economic reality that does not universalize the legitimate avenues by which such goods can be appropriated. In making this statement, it must be emphasized that such a resolution is by no means inevitable. Only a few young people respond to the predicament of unrealized and unrealizable consumption in the same way. Many poor people struggle through legitimate avenues such as education to accumulate the life chances that will allow them to become, as it were, 'normal consumers'. There are also other patterns of adaptation available to young people faced with this contradiction. Drug-taking and radical political mobilization, for example, represent other life opportunities that might not necessitate participation in street crime.

So far we have studied why young people wish to consume, and we have examined why alternative and illegal consumption strategies might be pursued. What we now need to consider is why some young people, and indeed a growing number of them, have chosen to drift in the direction of a consumption strategy that resolves itself into street crime. Why, we must ask, have they chosen to become flawed consumers? To accomplish this we must move from a consideration of structure towards an examination of process, in particular the diverse processes characteristic of what terms 'differential association' (Sutherland and Cressay 1979). We need to attend, in particular, to the social process by which allegiance to norms stressing adherence to rule-abiding behaviour become abandoned in favour of an alternative value system which encourages rule-breaking that embraces street crime.

I will argue that there are five factors we need to examine in order to explain how this process works.

- Though aware of condemnatory messages stigmatizing street crime, the messages young people receive are not consistent and can readily be ignored or circumvented.

- Proximity to and engagement with those who already break rules not only encourages this behaviour, but also sanctions participation in an outlaw culture that can actively celebrate and justify deviant values as a way of life.

- Street crime as an activity carries with it an array of seductions and benefits.

- Once engaged in street crime, young people can find it difficult to exit.

- There is a readily available stock of legitimations that permit rule-breaking to be excused or validated by bystanders and by participants.

Young people in Lambeth, like young people in British society, are products of an order that not only stigmatizes forms of rule-breaking such as street crime, but also imposes harsh penalties for those caught engaging in it. In the case of street crime, for example, a custodial sentence is a likely occurrence, and this can last for up to three years or more. Life is the maximum permitted tariff. Condemnation certainly exists, and condemnation is supported by an array of sanctions. And these, it should be emphasized, are almost always deployed against perpetrators apprehended through law-enforcement activity.

To understand why some young people turn to street crime as an adaptive strategy, we need to examine why they refuse to heed, or choose to ignore, wider messages of condemnation attached to this activity. To examine this issue, young offenders were asked an array of questions directed at ascertaining whether in fact they were aware of these condemnatory messages, and which also explored their moral perceptions more generally. In asking these questions, a number of subsidiary themes were also pursued. These related to the consistency of the messages of condemnation young people received; the appropriateness of the means by which they were mediated; how the messages were appropriated by the target audience; and how such messages related to the weight of non-condemnation they might receive from other bystanders.

While the young people evidently knew that street crime was wrong and was morally reprehensible, it was also evident that the messages they had received about crime were mixed and variable. The issue of street crime was rarely raised and discussed by parents, many of whom were surprised and upset when they subsequently found that their child had become involved as a perpetrator. All the young people interviewed claimed that schools did not provide much, if anything, in the way of information about street crime. Indeed, upon subsequent investigation, there was and remains no credible policy in schools on this issue.[1] Most of the young offenders had never been told much about how the criminal justice system worked, nor about what it would do to them if they were subsequently processed by it. Indeed, the only information about street crime they heard in the course of their schooling was that often provided through a single visit by a police officer. Time and again the words 'not knowing the consequences' or 'not thinking through the consequences' of acts were noted as a primary cause for involvement in robbery.

Though local community safety providers had embarked upon a media campaign, part of which was directed at warning young offenders about the consequences of offending, it was clearly lost upon its target audience. To a point this occurred because the message was not tested beforehand on those who were supposed to consume it. There was also the problem that no clear and consistent message was being delivered by anyone. What this vacuum has created, I will suggest, is a space in which other messages, specifically those that can come to sanction rule-breaking, can and have prospered.

With regard to the exposure of young people to messages that would encourage rule-abiding, as opposed to rule-breaking, behaviour, it was by no means evident that there was too much of this around. The role of organizations such as churches was entirely limited, given the secular and materialistic character of the world in which young people tend to live. While the free market can certainly encourage the will to consume – itself part of the problem – it must be emphasized that it offers no alternative morality or vision of the good life beyond the will to consume more. It is, in effect, an amoral entity. The pronouncements of other self-professed moral entrepreneurs such as politicians had no impact on the lives of these young men. They were perceived to embody a world that was distant and irrelevant to their lives. Nor could what they said be trusted. As with many forces of authority in their lives, such figures could easily be viewed as the enemy. Nor did political ideologies have much if any impact upon the conduct of these young men. To this extent they were certainly products of a postmodern depoliticized culture that had well and truly separated itself from older and more benevolent narratives of progress. Nor were there many remnants left of older working-class patterns of solidarity that might have induced their young into showing more respect for older traditional values. Capitalism's triumph at the 'end of history', as Fuketyama characterized the process, had successfully eliminated even these (Fuketyama 1992). In the era of unfettered competitive individualism, celebrated as a virtue in the free market, belt-and-braces socialism was well and truly starved of the oxygen that might once have nurtured it.

While much has been made by the media about the need for appropriate role models in young people's lives, what the interviews with young offenders revealed was that these young men tended to have none. If they did then it was often their parents, and in particular their mothers, which was itself an interesting insight because it clearly demonstrated how attached they were to traditional notions of family life. Leaving aside the arrogant assumption on the part of the adult world that youth should respect it more, it could also be remarked here that even if a positive role model could be identified, so too could plenty of others that wider society would not view in such terms. Among these, as we shall see, could be those who were successful practitioners of street crime and crime more generally.

For young people to become involved in street crime it is not enough that the voices that might condemn such behaviour go unheeded. Involvement in such activity is also contingent on being in contact with or in close proximity to what I will generically term outlaw groups who not only engage in rule-breaking, but who also inhabit a culture that justifies such activity and actively encourages it. As indicated above, while all young people are socialized to become active consumers of material goods, not all resolve problems of thwarted consumption by engagement in street crime. If we attend to those who do traverse this path, then it appears that at the very least they must:

- have witnessed street crime practised successfully by others around them;
- live in proximity to or actively socialize with those who practise it;
- have over time become active and confirmed members of these groups;
- have come to appreciate, as a consequence of successful engagement in street crime, the benefits such activity can deliver to their lives.

To engage in offences such as street crime, a person typically has to come into contact with those who already have some experience in its practice. It is not an activity that just occurs or simply happens. Like any other social activity, it requires skill and dexterity to practise well. It is an activity which is, I would argue in most cases, socially learnt. It also requires a certain social presentation of self, and a certain amount of planning and teamwork to accomplish. Successful practitioners must be competent in their capacity to demonstrate aggression and violence. They must be able to use violence if violence is required. Speed and agility are also prerequisites for initiating a successful robbery, as are the ability to plan escape routes and identify suitable target areas. In addition to the above, those who practise street crime must be able to inhabit a world where they can live easily with themselves.

The way in which contact with already offending groups was established differed in terms of its intensity. For some young people it could be that they had witnessed others successfully prosecuting street crime, who lived within the context of a culture whose values excused it, and who consequently sought to emulate such activity. Given the sheer volume of street crime in areas like Lambeth, it could be surmised that due to its prevalence most young people were placed in this situation. For the same reason, most would also be aware of successful street robbers around them, especially as many would openly flaunt the rewards of their enterprise and initiative. Most would also be familiar with and live in proximity to a cultural order in which street crime was perceived as an inescapable feature of social life. As one man said, 'Yes I've seen people getting robbed. I've seen my friends being robbed. There is lots of bad stuff around here.'

In conjunction with boredom (a regularly cited feature of some young people's lives), unrequited consumption desires and living with poverty, this conjunction of circumstance could on occasion provoke street crime as an adaptive opportunist strategy. One man explained how he became attracted to street robbery:

> When I was young I would say to my mum something like 'Can I have a pair of trainers?' and because my mum didn't work and was like on social security she could hardly put food on the table. And when I was young I would look at that and I would see other people making money, driving around in the latest cars and I would think 'There must be an easier way'.

As interviews with young offenders showed, the most likely gateway into street robbery lay not only in being part of a group that had observed it or living in a cultural milieu that excused it, but rather participation occurred through intensive exposure to outlaw groups that practised it. Just as Oliver Twist became an apprentice to Fagin and his gang, so too do putative street robbers require access to those who already possess the necessary skills, craft and experience. Not only is the proximity to actual offenders a necessary condition but, such proximity also functions as an alternative space in which deviant values and necessary criminal skills can be learnt, internalized and developed.

Again, the route-way into contact with such outlaw cultures could differ. It could occur because you grew up with people who belonged to outlaw groups, such as neighbours, friends or family members. It could occur because you moved into an area where members of such groups congregated or lived. It could also occur because you became friends with group members or wished to become accepted by them in a relation of friendship in order to achieve respect in their eyes or – and this could be important – to avoid the possibility of victimization at their hands. Contact could therefore arise as a consequence of a defensive strategy. While it might be tempting to view the decision to become involved with such groups in terms of an active choice made consciously, this would be to overstate a reality where the choices available are highly constrained. Spatially compressed into estates from which there were no realistic exit strategies, proximity and contact were, for most young offenders, inescapable features of their lives. As such, an important question many young people tended to face was not how to avoid contact with such groups, but how to do the kinds of things that would earn their respect. As we shall see, this could involve street crime.

One of the young men explained how he was initiated. He had, he explained, recently moved to Brixton, where he found himself something of a stranger on the local estate and in the proximity of an older group of boys who did street robbery and who put pressure on him to become involved. I asked him about the kind of pressure they placed on him.

> Like they would say, 'Are you coming out there?' and if you like said no, then they say 'You going to come along with us' and I would say no so they say 'You a pussy, you going to have to come with us'.

Another young man cited his exposure to a gang of older men (aged 19–21), all of whom were involved in illegal activity, specifically robbery and selling drugs. In his words:

> I started hanging round with some people in Brixton. I would see them everyday. I was with my friend and his older brother used to always do crime. And I would hang out with my friend and he would always try and be like his older brother and we would hang out with the gang as well and do stuff. And that's when we thought we would try it [robbery].

The element of peer pressure to engage in robbery was intense as the young man explained in relation to his first street robbery committed against an older man in Clapham.

> They (the older gang) were gerrying me on like to make sure I did it. Then after I did do it like they said 'He's one of us now' and after that they didn't say so much.

Where the analogy with Fagin ends is that the groups of offenders who inhabit these outlaw cultures do not approximate the Fagin model of an organized criminal gang. What we are often looking at here are looser associations, specifically composed of young men, all of whom will have offended and who consider offending behaviour to be an obligation. At the heart of these associations will be certain people who are more proficient and more motivated to offend than others. They are often likely to be older than the people around them, and many will have had their criminal status conferred by having been 'successfully' processed at some time or other by the criminal justice system. In the words of the young offenders interviewed for the purpose of this research, these were the 'bad-boys': an already existing population of highly motivated offenders, many of whom would already have served custodial sentences. There was, said one young man, 'no leadership thing'. These men are those who have already been labelled criminal by the wider society, and who have, as designated criminals, consequently internalized the label and accorded to it a number of positive con-notations. In effect, as a consequence of successful labelling processes conferred by the criminal justice system, there now exist a number of young men who quite happily accept and celebrate their outlaw status. They live the life, they walk the walk and they talk the talk. This came through powerfully in a conversation with a young man in his early 20s who had recently been released after serving a prison sentence for robbery. In response to how he felt he was perceived by those around him, he characterized their response as, 'Yes, it's a kind of respect in a way. Now, no matter what I do, even if I choose not to do crime, they respect me because I earned their respect by doing crime.' When I asked him about the friends he grew up with on the street, he laughed and admitted, 'Yes, most are in jail.'

Though quantifying precise numbers remains inherently difficult, it could be surmised that these outlaw associations are widespread, and are specifically active when legitimate employment avenues are blocked. As my research in Lambeth suggested, many were well-established on many estates. Group membership is often conferred by point of origin or proximity to a particular territory and by virtue of the fact that most of those who are involved in such associations have grown up together. They would have gone to the same schools and have the same friends. Interviews also indicated that the more confirmed members of these groups were those who were the oldest and who were also involved in a range of other illegal activities. In particular, they were likely to be connected with grey and illegal markets. They would know, for example, where to buy drugs to deal and who to market them to. They would also know who to fence stolen goods to and were often in contact with those who would commission them to appropriate certain objects: 20 mobile phones, for example, with this particular specification. When I asked one young man about these networks he said:

> Yes there are a lot of people who do stuff. It's like you with a friend and you met people and they maybe sell heroin and you're with someone else who knows someone else who knows someone else whose selling something.

The most accomplished of the 'bad-boys' also knew precisely what make to take and were very selective about what they chose to target. As one young man commented, 'He don't steal anything less than a 32-10. He wouldn't steal that. It's the newer phones. You don't steal anything less than you can sell for £200.'

What acted to reinforce the involvement of young men who found themselves in proximity to such associations was the way in which the focal concerns of the group often came to predominate over other more legal and legitimate attachments young people might have, such as their families. As one man explained, 'All you know about is your friends. You forget your family. Friends are all that matter.'

And another: 'It's like your friends are all there is and you don't think of the consequences.'

And another: 'When you got a set of friends and someone fights, you got to fight with them.'

And when they find themselves together, for example at a youth club: 'There you meet people and … someone suggests "Let's do this", and that's how things [crime] begin.'

Group membership also brings other positive benefits, specifically security in a dangerous world: 'When I'm with them no one like tries to trouble you. But when I am by myself then they would try and trouble me.'

In terms of the values celebrated within these outlaw groups, what we can observe is a hybrid subculture which is forged out of a symbiosis between activities celebrated in the wider society and those condemned by it. Where it joins with the wider order is in its celebration of conspicuous consumption, and the linking of acquisitive materialism with notions of status and standing, distinction and respect. Where it departs is in its pursuit of socially sanctioned consumption norms by illicit means that sanction violence and rule-breaking as a way of life. This orientation also goes hand in hand with a celebration of a world that is specifically gendered in its form. Typically, what we can observe here is a world in which a particular vision of masculinity is celebrated. This is one in which the capacity to practise violence is validated and where being tough commands respect. This is also a cultural order in which the capacity to assert physical self is celebrated as a valid marker of being a man. It is a social currency that commands respect and begets for its holder social distinction and honour. For the young men I interviewed, fighting was a recurrent feature of life in a world considered violent and dangerous. 'Yes, you have to fight all the time', said one young man, while another noted ruefully that even though he knew many people in

Brixton, 'There are still people out there you got to be careful of.' This vision of masculinity, moreover, reaches into the detail of life. It is there in the physical presentation of self to the world: it is evident in the clothes, in the language, in the walk, and in speech itself. It is evident in acts and deeds, in what is spoken about, and what is celebrated in speech.

The gendered character of this world-view is evident not only in what it selects as worthy of celebration, but also in what it has to deny in the process of its own becoming. The vision of purified masculinity that it celebrates is often brought about at the cost of disavowing much of what wider society has chosen to endorse. This can include the idea that worldly success can be established through hard work at school, or that self-respect can be accomplished through entry into the legitimate job market. Often the way in which this disavowal is socially demonstrated is by coding such activity as explicitly feminized behaviour. Working hard at school or demonstrating intellectual effort are perceived as unmanly, as something that real men do not do. This could lead some young men actively to preclude themselves from mainstream society and work in the formal economy (Willis 1977). As one young man observed: 'They don't want it [work]. They ain't looking for it.'

This gendered perception is also associated with a disavowal of what society itself codes as feminine: this can include being overtly emotional, intimating care and evincing compassion for others. Unsurprisingly, the kind of culture this produces and the kind of individual it sanctions is not well equipped to interact with society on its preferred terms. What it sanctions is a form of 'lawless masculinity' (Cambell 1993), evident in males unable to resolve conflict without recourse to aggression, and who are often homophobic and sexist in their behaviour. This kind of individual is, however, well-equipped and motivated to practise street crime and engage in criminal behaviour more generally. Such individuals, once confirmed within the rituals of outlaw culture, not only reproduce it, but can actively induct other young people into it as well.

The culture of aggressive masculinity discussed above is not unique to Lambeth or indeed to any specific ethnic group. Criminologists have explored variations of it in different countries and between different groups (Willis 1977; Cambell 1993). In content it remains quite consistent over time and between states. It does, however, manifest itself via a number of stylistic variations which distinguish various outlaw cultures from each other. The social rituals it practices may vary, as might its stylistic expression, for instance through the style of clothes, music etc.

In the case of its instantiation in Lambeth, the social conditions described above have created an ideal environment in which such outlaw cultures can thrive. In terms of the way it is grounded in the culture of street criminals, particularly among certain young black males, it is evident in the social presentation to the world that borrows heavily from the hip-hop, gangster rap culture of the United States. This influence is particularly evident in physical presentation of self to the world. It is evident in the aggressive assertion of self that can often be observed in the way young men move. It is there in the loose-fitting trousers worn as if hanging off the crotch; it is there in the way they express themselves in their body language and through the sign language they use to communicate. Unsurprisingly, many of these stylistic features had their origin in the penitentiary culture associated with the US punitive mass incarceration policy. Baggy trousers and unlaced shoes, for example, derive from prison uniforms, while the sign language evolved as a mode of communication among inmates in an institutional context in which silence was often policy.[2]

As subcultural theorists observe, the social rituals attached to outlaw cultures are both complex and highly creative (Hebdige 1979; Hall 1976). In effect, they produce and reproduce a culture that consciously aspires to define itself away from a dominant order, which it confronts in a stance of hostility and often aggression. Such cultures work, however, precisely because they confer many benefits on their members. Against a society which provides them with little in the way of life chances, it provides an alternative and parallel set of opportunities to appropriate what the wider society holds out as desirable but simultaneously denies. Against an order that provides little by way of market opportunity, it offers the possibility of work – though of an illegal kind. Like the formal economy, it also offers on-site training. Against an emerging economy where the work provided is often menial, low-paid and of a nine-to-five variety, it offers work opportunities which can gain you peer respect, while providing you with the means to gratify material desires in a much quicker time frame than the formal job market allows. As a number of young men pointed out, in an economy that paid only £3.50 per hour, street crime was an entirely rational career move. It could generate over £150 for less than an hour's work. As one man put it, 'When you is young and you realize that you can make over a thousand and ten pounds in half an hour, you going to do the half hour.' And another: 'It's easy money'.

Finally, if in the low-wage 'mac-economy', where the only work available was likely to be dull, repetitious, monotonous and boring, that provided by the counterculture stressed values celebrated by many young people, including the possibility of risk, thrills and danger.

What also sustains these cultures as viable enterprises is that they can individually and collectively help sustain alternative economies in areas characterized by high levels of deprivation and poverty. In effect, street crime can be viewed as an economic enterprise that is itself part of a large black-market economy (Sutton 1995). In the case of Lambeth, this market included drugs, people and, not least, the proceeds of street crime. Like all successful economies, this economy possesses a complex division of labour. Some participated within it as primary suppliers of goods and services that other consumers, such as drug-users, or those looking to make cheap purchases off the back of the proverbial lorry, would then buy. There are also a lot of middlemen engaged in this industry, including those who help purchase stolen goods and provide retail outlets through which these goods can be moved on. According to the testimony of offenders, a number of shops and stores in Lambeth performed this role. Offenders also mentioned shadowy figures that would commission illegal acts. The more confirmed young people became in various outlaw cultures, the more knowledge they would accumulate about how the illegal market economy operated. With this in mind, I would suggest that if we want to offer another reason why Lambeth has such a high crime rate, then this can in part be explained by reference to the size, strength and vitality of this economy. Street crime, it might be said, not only flourishes because the formal economy cannot universalize the means to consume legally, but it also rises because there is already an alternative economy to sustain it.

If we now look at what Katz (Katz 1988) refers to as the 'seductions of being evil', then the pleasures attendant on being involved in street crime and the subculture that sanctions it become more obvious. In the act of street robbery, a power relation is forged between the violent aggressor and the victim. In the assertion of power through violence, a form of pleasure can also be accessed on the part of the perpetrator: specifically, the pleasure in power. For those who typically inhabit a social order that confers little of this, this is by no means a minor issue. If we examine the phenomenology of street crime more closely, other pleasures can also be observed. Though for the wider society the act might well look like a form of cowardice, from the standpoint of perpetrators the act can have other connotations. To knowingly break rules that command severe penalties if caught can take courage. Not least, a certain existential abyss has to be crossed. Can you make the grade? Do you have what it takes? Then there is the status and respect that you can accrue in participating in the act. The respect that will be accorded to you by others, specifically those already engaged in street crime and other offences: your direct peer group. This fact came through recurrently in the way involvement in street robbery was represented in interview as a kind of initiation ceremony; a right of passage into the outlaw culture wherein you become a (mostly) man of respect in a world where respect is everything and where being 'a pussy', as one man put it, was unthinkable.

As contact with victims was often very fleeting, the act of street crime was characterized by a social distance between victim and perpetrator which meant that the latter would have little opportunity to think of the victim in anything approaching human terms. Street crime, it could be observed, is a very dehumanizing act. Finally, having successfully prosecuted street crime, you could then openly display to others the results of your labour. Many apparently do. Given a cultural order of street values beholden to a norm that holds you never inform to the police, it is easy to see how this tendency can flourish. The active threat of violence that would invariably be directed at those who violate this principle also reinforces it.

As a number of young offenders interviewed for this project testified, the peer pressure they faced to commit street crime was intense. In effect, it became a rite of passage for many into the order of the outlaw culture on whose fringes they may have found themselves for reasons explained earlier. In participation you received the respect of your peers and also – and this was significant – lowered the likelihood of being coded as a victim: as someone, that is, who could be judged as a target either of robbery or of violence. In the act your status as a man was in effect socially demonstrated and validated in action. In street crime there was also a sense expressed that you were getting one over on 'them', the wider society, and not least the police whose efforts to catch you, you were able to avoid. This fact was attested to a number of times in the interviews. Often the terms of this discussion were polarized in terms of the perceived fitness, agility and cunning of the street robber, and the unfit, pondering and dull reflexes of law-enforcement officers. That young men who had actually been caught were responsible for this testimony was rather ironic, not least because it was clear that their thesis had been disconfirmed in the act of their arrest.

In street crime, young men were also accorded the means to achieve an autonomy and self-reliance they otherwise found it difficult to obtain, given their limited capacity to enter the formal labour market. Often acutely aware that their families could not afford to provide them with the material goods they had been taught to covet, a number considered such activity in cold instrumental terms as a viable means by which they could provide for themselves. In a state of prolonged adolescence provided by limited market opportunities and mass youth unemployment, such independence could be viewed as providing a gateway to adulthood more generally.

Finally, in street crime another benefit can also be observed which raises it above participating in other forms of offence such as burglary. For those who had acquired the right skills, it was easy to commit and the risk of being apprehended was slight. In relation to other possible illegal activities, street crime also conferred more advantages which have cumulatively acted to make it the most favoured form of crime. To commit financial 'scams' required equipment and expertise most young people did not have access to. For similar reasons, the gateway to more lucrative forms of white-collar crime was also denied to these predominantly young working-class men. Exclusions from the formal labour market, it could be observed, are also reproduced in the illegal market. Given that most developments in 'community crime control' in the last two decades have concentrated on situational prevention measures evident in target-hardening of fixed targets such as shops, homes and cars (Clarke 1980), the effect of this has been to render such targets harder to attack. Such enhanced defences also make detection more likely. The turn to street crime can thus be seen as an entirely rational response to an overall reduction in target availability. If we now connect this observation with the rise of populations of suitable victims, then it is self-evident why street crime has been such a growth industry.

An important phase in the process of differential association lay in the difficulties that people who have become engaged as perpetrators in street crime face in returning to a law-abiding existence. First, in acquiring the skills to commit street crime – not least the capacity to demonstrate physical aggression – young men, in particular, confirm the drift towards a form of aggressive masculinity that can further confirm their participation in an outlaw culture. The problem here is that in becoming such a male they have to purify themselves through disavowal of other qualities that permit alternative and positive associations with the wider society. They can also assume a fully outlaw status and this can become integral to their identity.

If they get caught and are processed by the criminal justice system, though this might well be the preferred vehicle through which societal displeasure is evidenced, the process can also have the effect of confirming their criminal status by formally conferring on them a criminal label. Being processed in this way, it might be added, has a number of other consequences. Firstly, being processed through custodial institutions does not carry a street stigma on the part of those who have been processed this way. It can and often is worn as a marker of respect. Second, it is also a process in which young men can and do acquire an enhanced set of criminal skills. Thirdly, when young men are released back into society their life chances are so reduced that participation in crime becomes their only viable option. As a research project conducted by the local probation service in Lambeth found, the living conditions for many offenders could only be described as chaotic.

The final factor that is important in sustaining a culture conducive to the production of motivated offenders ready and willing to commit street crime is that the desire to break rules in this way can easily be sanctioned. This can happen both by those who break them and by onlookers as well. As the work of Sykes (1957) and more recently Cohen (Cohen 2001) has shown, one reason why people break rules and continue to do so is that they can deploy various techniques of neutralization to justify what they do. These techniques can take a number of forms, and involve the creation of plausible narratives that can act to justify rule-breaking or inaction in confronting it. In Lambeth, one such narrative was that young people were engaged in a kind of Robin Hood existence: stealing from the rich and giving to the poor. Another was that in street crime young black people were engaged in 'resistance' to white racist culture.

In conclusion, in our consideration of the production of motivated offenders we have examined the background structural factors that create the underlying causes that produce the will to offend. In exploring this issue we have examined why young people have come to covet and desire the goods that are stolen. We have also examined why general socio-economic conditions conspire to produce a situation in which a number of young people will come to choose illegal as opposed to legal consumption strategies. Finally, we have traced a number of more proximate factors whose conjunction favours a drift into an outlaw existence in which street crime can be sanctioned as legitimate.

Notes

1 Which was strangely ironic, because in the meetings I convened with them the headteachers were adamant that the environments they provided for young people were bastions of morality and good citizenship.
2 The relation between the gangster hip-hop look and US penitentiary culture was explained to the author by D. Brotherton.

Chapter 9

Deficits in social control

As with any other offence, street robbery is perpetrated in the context of attempts by various control agents to prevent it. To study why an offence such as street robbery has risen in recent years, it is therefore important to study why the range of interventions that society imposes to prevent this offence have not worked. In addition to studying the dyad between offenders and victims – examined in the previous two chapters – we must also consider the various deficits in social control which have not prevented motivated offenders from preying on their victims.

As the discussion in Chapter 6 indicated, there are potentially a number of ways to address this issue. For the purpose of this analysis, however, I will cut the control cake into four slices, the failures of which I will address in turn. I will begin by examining the role of the *police*, the front-line agency most people logically assume to play the single most important role in confronting offences like street robbery. I will then consider the *judicial response* to street robbery, and will do so by examining the effectiveness of the various sanctions and interventions society has chosen to deliver to those offenders apprehended by the police. I will then examine the performance of those who have embraced *situational crime prevention* as a crime control strategy, a perspective that has in recent decades come to assume an ever more important role in the prevention of crime more generally in free-market societies. Finally, I will consider the impact of what I will loosely term *social crime-prevention initiatives*, a general expression for attempts to prevent crime by rectifying the social conditions that are held to give rise to it.

Collectively these interventions include reactive responses geared to intervening to address the problem of street crime after it has occurred, as well as more proactive interventions that may be understood to perform a role in preventing the problem. Typically, the former are more likely to include the efforts of law-enforcement agencies and the judicial interventions mediated through the activities of the criminal justice system. The latter embody a range of social strategies that, while not specifically crime-related, can also impact on crime by preventing young people from becoming motivated offenders.

In addition to examining these four crime-prevention control strategies, I will also look at the way in which this control effort is coordinated and integrated. I will examine in this sense the *management of crime prevention*, in addition to studying the performance of control agents pursuing different control strategies. A consideration of this issue is essential for two reasons. Firstly, because increasing the efficiency of crime-control agents through subjugating them to managerialist imperatives is now seen in itself as an important crime-prevention strategy. Secondly, and on a more obvious note, self-evidently the ways in which 'responsible authorities' coordinate and direct community safety at the local level can be considered to perform an important role in confronting street robbery.

Policing

When the media and politicians debate the street crime problem, it is typically to the police that they and everyone else tend to look for solutions and, not least, quick results. As the police have also traditionally been more than happy to accept this role, this has only managed to confirm such expectations in everyone's minds. An inevitable consequence of this is that it places the police under immense pressure to deliver results and to deliver them quickly. Which is all very well if (a) they are prepared and (b) they can respond quickly to the problem. Faced with a real and sharp escalation in street robbery in the late 1990s, however, it was clear that they were neither prepared nor were able to respond rapidly and convincingly to address the problem. In fact, it would not be an underestimation to suggest that they were totally unprepared for the rise in street robbery with the consequence that, as media coverage intensified, they found themselves the subject of an intense critique from both the media and the government.

To account for their own failure, the police originally blamed the sharp and sudden escalation in street robbery on the aftereffects of the September 11 atrocities in the US. In the face of the terror threat, security had to be considerably enhanced, with the result that resources that were usually deployed on the streets were used instead for anti-terrorism purposes. At the centre of this argument was the contention that street robbery rates only increased because suitable guardians were not in place to defend the good society. As Fitzgerald *et al.* argue, however, there are two key problems with this argument. Firstly, the rise in street robbery preceded the events of September 11; secondly, if police stop-and-search over this period can be read as an index of police activity on the streets, then this did not change over the period where it was claimed police resources were being redirected. In effect, the argument simply does not stand up to close inspection (Fitzgerald *et al.* 2002).

Two important conclusions follow through from this. The first is that street robbery actually increased at a time when there were no real changes in the methods the police typically deployed to confront it, and, secondly, at a time when the resources used to confront it remained largely the same. One implication of this is that police activity as such was not that important a driver in accounting for rising street robbery which has, as we have seen in previous chapters, other social causes. This does not, however, mean that police activity is insignificant or un-important. I would suggest that what rising street robbery indicated was that the resources deployed to confront the problem were incapable of addressing the sudden escalation, while the tactics traditionally used were not particularly successful in preventing it. These limitations, however, did not begin to become apparent until the rise in street robbery actually occurred.

If we now consider the limits of policing as a street robbery prevention strategy, a number of points could be made. To begin with, given inherently finite human resources, and, in the case of high-crime boroughs such as Lambeth, significantly overstretched resources, the police cannot be everywhere at once and consequently cannot provide a comprehensive security canopy. They cannot, in other words, police every street on a 24 hour basis, given that they do not have the capability to do so. As street crime rises typically from 3.00pm onwards, so do other calls on police time. This reduces the human resources available to address street crime effectively at the very point when more resources are required. In addition to these structural constraints, the police also face the inherently difficult task of trying to be in the right place at the right time in a world where the people they are doing their best to apprehend are also doing their best to avoid them.

While police presence, particularly in high-crime areas, can act as a visual deterrent as well as providing symbolic reassurance to the public, it also produces as a consequence a corresponding rise in street crime elsewhere, as street robbers, heedful of the control effort, move their activities to other areas. This could either be in the form of spatial or temporal displacement patterns, and both have been regularly observed in areas like Lambeth. As the police have also found, if effort is subsequently scaled back within a targeted zone, in order, for example, to target new and emerging hot spots, then the problem of street crime also has a habit of returning.

Most crimes that are solved by the police typically follow from information provided by the public (Lea and Young 1984). Though the police do receive useful intelligence from the public that enables them to detect those involved in street crime, there are a number of factors that clearly limit the quality and quantity of the information they receive. First, insensitive policing styles in the past have acted to create a situation characterized by poor police/community relations. In many areas where street robbery is high, this legacy still lingers among certain sections of the local community despite changes in policing styles. As a recent community safety survey in Lambeth indicated, while most local residents showed a high degree of trust in police performance overall, the black population of respondents were less likely to trust the police than other population groups (Hallsworth and MaGuire 2002). Of the populations that had actually used the police services black victims were far less likely than other population groups to feel that they had been treated well.

Young people also find themselves socialized into a culture in which the police tend to be negatively perceived. As young offenders in Lambeth intimated in interviews conducted for the purpose of this research, it was not that they hated the police as individuals, but rather that they had no language available to consider them in anything other than a negative way. They were simply the 'feds', and their mission in life was to drive around in 'bully-vans' with the purpose of harassing young people. While police tactics such as stop-and-search certainly reinforced this perception, it was also evident that young people in the borough are also aware of and subject to a cultural injunction that holds that no information should or ought to be made available to the police. This culture of silence is also sustained and reproduced by the threat of real violence should anyone choose to transgress this principle.

An important consequence that followed through from the failure of existing police tactics to confront rising street robbery was that the police and the police effort itself became quickly discredited in the eyes of young and active street robbers. The young offenders in Lambeth, for example, manifested a high degree of disrespect for a law-enforcement system they viewed with contempt and which they believed they could quite literally run rings around. Indeed, being able to escape from the clutches of the 'feds' could be appropriated as a form of symbolic capital to command respect among a peer group. The failure of the police to bring street robbery under control thus weakened the credibility of social control agents, which in turn fuelled the rise in street crime further.

In considering the role of police performance, specifically in high-crime areas like Lambeth, a number of other factors also need to be considered. All inner-city areas pose more problems for the police than rural or suburban areas. In the case of Lambeth, these problems have been accentuated historically by a legacy of poor police/community relations and a history of urban disorder in the 1980s (Scarman 1981). Lambeth, according to the Metropolitan Police's own regulatory authority, is recognized as being among the most difficult areas to police in western Europe. While community relations have improved remarkably in the last few years, not least as a consequence of a range of initiatives led by the borough's (then) innovative police commander Paddick, imposing the rule of law in such areas is by no means easy to achieve. One problem concerns the form of policing that would be considered acceptable to the wider community in an era when their representatives are now actively consulted. As one officer observed, while active consultation had certainly improved community relations, it did so, at a cost to the police of not being able to deploy all the coercive powers at their disposal. Another issue concerns the probable impact on areas like Brixton if strong-arm tactics were to be used. Order on the streets is always, it should be noted, a negotiated affair. Enforcing control through coercive law and order means alone remains problematic, not least because community memories are long and disorder remains a real possibility. While reclaiming the streets from street robbers consequently remains a police priority, it is evident that police attempts to accomplish this have to occur in ways that ensure recent gains in their relationship with the wider community are not prejudiced.

Punishment

Though the police are often seen as the key institution in the fight against street crime, the role of the judicial system and the organizations that support it must also be considered of fundamental importance. Cumulatively, these bodies perform a number of important functions. In the act of punishment dispensed to offenders, a message is sent out to the public that they have erred and should desist from further offending. To ensure that offenders who have been caught understand the deterrent message they have received, they are also subjected to a range of interventions designed to ensure that they are rehabilitated, or at least that the risk they are held to pose is managed.

The sanctions that the state deploys to deter and punish those guilty of street crime can range from benign forms of intervention, evident in community sanctions delivered through referral orders, through to what may be regarded as harsh and punitive custodial sentences. With the formation of Youth Offending Teams, the New Labour government initiated the formation of local multiagency crime-prevention bodies whose principal aim has been to prevent offending by young people under 18. While the aim of intervention for under-18s is towards non-custodial solutions, detention orders are also often deployed for this age group in the case of street crime because of its association with violence.

For those over 18 charged with street crime, the sentence is almost always custodial and often lasts for around 3 years, a penalty no doubt reflecting the government's desire to be seen to be 'tough on crime'. Whether or not the offence was first-time made little difference to the way offenders were treated, as we found in our research in Lambeth using local data supplied by the probation service. Ethnicity did, however, as 96 per cent of young black males received custodial sentences, as opposed to 68 per cent for the white population. The ferocity underpinning this punitive response, it could also be noted, made the tariff for street robbery far higher in the area than that for assault, according to the same data.

As to whether this get-tough policy is appropriate and useful, a number of fairly critical observations could be made. First, if the aim of the punitive response was to deter street crime, then self-evidently it has failed, as the rising tide of street crime offences testify. Second, it is very expensive, as the bill for incarcerating young people is over £35,000 per year per offender, according to Home Office figures. Third, from research conducted among young offenders, it was evident that far from significantly reducing the will to offend on the part of those receiving custodial sentences, prison appeared to have had the opposite effect. Recidivism rates remain at around 60 per cent, and, according to the testimony of young people, far from the experience acting to prevent crime, it placed them in a context where they were able to learn a number of new techniques to prosecute it.

If we accept, as I argued earlier, that street crime is a behaviour that is learnt, then, as interviews with young offenders testified, many of the people they learnt their skills from, or who they hoped to impress, were those who had already been processed through the penal system. Far from preventing street crime, it could be argued that the current array of judicial solutions, in their coercive form at least, exacerbate the very problem they are supposed to prevent, in this case by returning young men to their community as fully confirmed career criminals. As one man observed when I asked about how his colleagues viewed him when he had been released, 'Yes I say I got respect.'

If the aim of the judicial interventions to which young offenders were subjected was designed to make them rethink their criminal behaviour, their treatment at the hands of the judiciary often made this aim difficult to realise in practice. To begin with, the timescale involved in disposing of offenders often meant that the distance between their arrest and their prosecution and eventual sentencing could run into months. It could also be characterized by a number of delays. Far from this process making offenders question their crimes, it would often appear to generate a sense of anger and heighten an already high level of distrust and animosity. As street robbers quickly realize prison is their inevitable destination, their time on remand can often be viewed as one of preparation and not least socialization to its rituals. Given that many street criminals quickly become aware of what the judicial system has in store for them, this also affects the way they view the white middle-class elites who typically dispense justice. Far from seeing them as legitimate representatives of a law whose application they respect, the response is often simply to extend the proverbial middle finger on the basis that everything is a foregone conclusion anyway.

As to their time spent inside prison, from the interviews conducted it was by no means evident that the experience was particularly redemptive in its outcome. As a number of offenders pointed out, getting used to prison life was not difficult, and while its rituals were not necessarily pleasant, they did confront the often aimless world of the incarcerated young men with routines to which they could readily adapt. As an offender remarked, 'You don't have to worry about food, paying your bills, or having to find a job. They do it for you.' All they had to do was mind their business and do their best to avoid the endemic violence that often characterized these harsh and austere institutions. Learning to conform to rituals, however, is not the same thing as becoming a reformed individual, and rituals alone do not provide for this.

As the prisons to which these young men were sent were often a considerable distance from their homes, and as it is common prison practice to shift prisoners between prisons, life inside also meant considerable separation from their families and care workers. As offenders are often seriously alienated from mainstream society and consequently from the web of interdependencies that characterize normal social life, this systemically practised rite of exclusion also works to intensify further their alienation more generally. All of which makes the task of reclaiming these young men much more difficult. As one said, 'Prison, it don't teach you nothing.' And another, 'I was only inside four days and I learnt more crime inside than outside.' When pressed on this he spoke of how he had been taught to hot-wire a car.

When offenders were asked to specify if they could identify a moment when they were forced to confront the consequences of what they had done, then almost every young person I interviewed remarked that this occurred when they had to confront their parents, specifically their mothers. As one young man remarked when I asked him if there was a moment when he found himself questioning his involvement in robbery, 'Seeing my mother in tears. I don't want to see her that way again'. This was a point at which guilt appeared to be real. What the judges who sentenced them generated was less a feeling of guilt so much as fear. To be told you face a prison sentence was registered as a powerful existential moment in their lives. 'To be told you are going down ... that was scary.' As the judicial bureaucratic juggernaut to which these young men were now attached moved inexorably forward, however, and as the professionals took control, the potential redemptive lesson the young could have derived from this became lost. As professionals are not people with whom young offenders may readily identify, and as the language and rituals of the judicial domain remain opaque to their experience, the system offers little opportunity or space to make offenders question their criminal activity. As to the population of people before whom they could be placed and whose opinions they might be more likely to respect – namely representatives from their own community – then these have no stake in the system at all. In effect, they remain excluded from participation in the provision of justice altogether. Not only does this further alienate the offender, but it also acts to alienate the public from conflicts in which they have a stake: it's their children after all who get prosecuted and sent to prison. Another negative implication is that in their exclusion, local communities become further alienated from community safety providers, which in turn propels them to embrace, as everyone does, the myth that the police can solve the problem of street crime alone.

Situational crime prevention

Recent decades have borne witness to the creation of a new form of criminology. By nature it is pragmatic, rational and instrumental in orientation. Far from seeking grand solutions to the causes of crime, it operates instead by seeking to discover technical solutions to specific problems by attempting to design environments or goods in ways that minimize the threat posed by crime in their area. Championed by the Home Office in the 1980s, this form of criminology is known as situational crime prevention (Clarke 1980). It is currently one of the most important crime-prevention tools used by local community safety providers. If we examine how situational crime prevention measures impact upon street crime, we will see that its results are variable. More specifically, I would suggest that:

- Forms of situational crime prevention used to protect fixed targets have helped make street crime more attractive to motivated offenders.

- The form of situational crime prevention that has been widely deployed to help prevent street crime has been largely ineffective.

- Forms of situational crime prevention that might have been applied to 'target harden' consumable goods targeted by street robbers have not been developed or deployed. In other words, what might have worked has not been initiated.

If we examine where most situational crime prevention effort has been concentrated, then research suggests that most has been directed at 'target hardening' the built environment. New buildings, for example, are designed in ways that take into account issues of situational defence and come, as it were, already hardened. They consequently come complete with an array of design features that are specifically designed to render them burglar-proof. In the case of commercial premises such as shops, this can include sophisticated alarm systems, burglar-proof locks, camera surveillance, and steel shutters that fortify the building when it is closed. The attempt to design out crime also extends much further than single buildings, and can include entire built environments such as shopping centres and corporate business districts. The use of this approach also extends to the way products such as cars are designed.

Cumulatively, the impact of these initiatives has been to help reduce crime selectively by reducing the availability of lucrative targets. Statistically, the success of this enterprise can be seen in the falling rate of burglary and car crime, and by the relatively low level of crime identified in intensively fortified areas. In the case of Canary Wharf, for example, a heavily defended retail/business area in London, crime rates within its jurisdiction are minimal.

Paradoxically, an unforeseen circumstance of this strategy, I would suggest, has been to make offences such as street robbery far more likely, particularly in areas such as Lambeth. The reason for this is that street criminals are not stupid, as we have seen. They weigh up the relative costs and benefits associated with crime and many have come to the conclusion that street crime is less difficult to prosecute than burglary and there is little chance of detection. In addition, being young and poor, they are unable to accumulate, as they also pointed out in interviews, the necessary resources to initiate more lucrative financial 'scams' or become involved in white-collar crime more generally.

If we now consider the situational measures that have been adopted to confront street crime, these have principally centred around installing an intensive array of CCTV cameras. Though originally located across shopping precincts, current moves are also afoot to extend their deployment into many of the local housing estates. In pursuing this path, it should be emphasized local crime prevention partnerships are following a strategy that is not only popular across the county, but a strategy well-supported and funded by the government and the Home Office. As a strategy it is also an experiment in crime control that is quite unique to the UK. Other European countries and the United States, have not embraced CCTV to anything like the same extent.

While the use of CCTV has been proven to have some impact on crime rates, its utility as a street crime prevention tool is by no means proven. Motivated offenders do consider issues such as where cameras are situated when they plan their crimes, and consequently ensure that many of their victims are targeted outside the scan-scape of the cameras. Cumulatively the hydraulic effect of this is once again to shift street crime elsewhere rather than diminish its prevalence. More disturbingly, it would appear from the testimony of the young offenders interviewed that they had also become well aware of the limits of CCTV as a detection device. This was tied to their observation that its quality was often so bad that even if a crime was caught on the camera, law-enforcement agencies would not be able to recognize anyone from the footage. As one young man observed when he was shown pictures of a street robbery taken with CCTV, 'They [the police] told me it was me. But I didn't recognize nobody. I didn't even recognize myself.' Street robbers also learnt from experience that they were so fleet of foot that they would be long gone before the camera observers could call upon law-enforcement agencies to intervene.

Where situational attempts to design out street crime might have worked, these have not been initiated. If mobile phones – perhaps the single most important object of desire to street robbers – had been designed in ways that made them more difficult to use, then self-evidently they would not be stolen. The corporate producers of this technology, however, did not consider or ignored the criminogenic consequences of their technology, and this error was compounded in turn by government failure to regulate the industry. This might be considered odd, because the lessons of failing adequately to consider such issues have been well-known for a long time to the Home Office, as the case of car crime indicates.

Social crime prevention

The responses to street crime considered so far relate to attempts to address the problem either by preventing already motivated offenders from going about their unlawful business or by dealing with them once they have offended and have been caught. In this section I am going to consider various social attempts to prevent young people from becoming motivated offenders in the first place. The kind of strategies that would fall within this form of intervention would include:

- Attempts to warn and inform young people about the dangers and moral consequences of rule-breaking.

- Providing activities so that young people can sublimate their urges in more socially benevolent ways.

- Increasing the life chances of young people and their families in ways that reduce the forms of exclusion and deprivation that constitute the structural basis of street crime as an adaptive strategy.

Social attempts to prevent crime can take more ostensibly criminological forms in so far as they are characterized by a conscious attempt to reduce criminal behaviour through a particular policy. They may also be non-criminological in design but nevertheless play a key crime-reduction role. Attempts to provide information to young people about crime, for example, would be an instance of the former, while using regeneration funding to support marginal communities might be considered an example of the latter. In what follows, using the three broad characterizations of social crime prevention outlined above, we will consider how each functions to reduce offending behaviour in general and street crime in particular. As with the earlier discussions in this chapter, I will use the situation in Lambeth as a case study.

While young offenders claimed in interviews that they were aware street crime was a bad thing to do, they nevertheless came to do it anyway and growing numbers of young people appear to be making the same choice – as rising rates of street crime testify. While they had internalized part of the message the wider society would have wanted them to register (that street crime was a bad thing), evidently many young men had not received the message in a way that meant anything substantially to the choices they made. If we examine why, then we need to attend clearly to a number of problems evident in the content of the messages that are mediated, how crime-prevention messages are mediated and those responsible for mediating them.

If we consider what anti-street crime messages are mediated, the first observation that can be made is that those disseminated to young people were not mediated in a clear or consistent way. The reason for this would appear to be that the borough, as with the wider society, had no clear or coherent policy. To this could be added the observation that the dissemination of such messages was considered the sole business of parents and guardians and, in an uncoordinated and secondary role, teachers in schools. Because there is no clear and coherent agreement between the various stakeholders in the area about what such a strategy should be, no consistent message or information has been provided. The upshot of this is that each school adopts a more or less go-it-alone policy on the issue of crime prevention, and outside periodic visits by police officers to the schools who deign to admit them, there is no consistent crime-prevention message.

The outcome of this is that young people are often left with little understanding of the criminal justice system, how it operates, or what it will do to them if they break the law and are caught. They also know little about what happens to victims who are victimized, or what happens when weapons are used in events like armed robbery. Though schools certainly have anti-bullying policies, they are not consistent with one another. Evidence from the interviews conducted with young offenders also suggests that young people are not provided with the information that would allow them to access the criminal justice system when they themselves are victimized. Most young people are highly suspicious of involving the adult world anyway, on the basis that this would provoke more problems for the future.

While the decision motivated offenders make to target victims will occur independently of whether or not the local authority provides an array of more gainful activities, the provision of such services still remains important, not least to multiply deprived and disadvantaged young people most at risk of becoming involved in street crime. First, the provision of a wide and comprehensive set of activities for young people can be viewed as part of a process of social investment in young people's lives, independent of other reasons that might be used to justify it. They deserve to be able to have designated safe and interesting areas in which to play, and an array of leisure and social activities they can pursue if they so desire. Such spaces also provide opportunities for implicit educational messages to be mediated – including anti-crime messages. By engaging in activities with others, including other young people and adults, positive ties of interdependence can be encouraged that may act to offset the alienating and anomic tendencies of the wider free-market society.

Like many boroughs in London, the state of the youth service in areas like Lambeth and, not least, its contribution to community safety effort remains questionable. It is certainly not able in its current form to perform the crime-prevention role outlined above. There are a number of reasons that may be posited to account for this. First, in common with other boroughs, the idea of a youth service organized around the comprehensive provision of youth clubs has been questioned and abandoned. Second, this questioning has gone hand in hand with a series of sustained budget cuts that have literally decimated the forms of provision the council did operate or support. Third, in the face of financial retrenchment, the local authority has responded by effectively off-loading responsibility for youth provision onto a voluntary sector ill-equipped to undertake the infrastructure support role now being foisted upon it. Fourth, given access to inherently limited and precarious funding regimes, those seeking to work productively with young people are forced to engage in 'beauty competitions' in order to sustain often minimal funding for their activities.

While by no means decrying the activities of those who do provide services for young people, questions also need to be posed as to whether the services meet the needs of all their potential consumers and fulfil what may be considered a relevant community safety role. While organiza-tions such as the scouts, guides, army and navy cadets and woodcraft folk are worthy and continue to attract a population of young people, it is by no means evident that their appeal is particularly great to high-risk populations in deprived areas – the populations, in other words, most at risk of becoming engaged in street crime. Though recognizing that new spaces in place of old youth clubs need to be constructed, there remain few bold experiments that are orientated towards constructing such environments. Many of the kinds of activities that high-risk groups might value such as gyms, access to studios and electronic music equipment are either lacking or remain prohibitively expensive – as young offenders pointed out in interviews.

If we consider street crime as an adaptive strategy to thwarted consumption, and thwarted consumption as a function of real and rising patterns of relative deprivation in the borough, then self-evidently an important crime-reduction strategy must lie in reducing these factors. If we look at the social policies that might help to achieve this pattern of reduction, these are embraced within the general rubric of social regeneration measures that have been deployed in the last two decades. Though the crime-reducing aspect was not a principal aim of social regeneration, in recent years this function has increased dramatically. In fact, regeneration effort is often spoken of as if it were a *de facto* crime-prevention strategy (Hancock 2003). While headline figures attest to the inward investment of substantial sums of money to inner-city areas where street crime is high, it is by no means clear that the way spending priorities have been established has actually helped to reduce street crime. Indeed, I will show how the uneven regeneration that was attempted in Lambeth actually contributed significantly to its rising street crime problem.

As a precursor to this, however, it is worth noting the amount of regeneration expenditure that has flowed into the borough since the urban disorders of the 1980s. As the partial list below indicates, the sums involved are substantial:

- Single Regeneration Budget £250 million (1994–2007)
- Housing £169 million (1998–2002)
- Health Action Zone £25 million (1998–2005)
- Education Action Zone £3 million (1998–2002)
- New Deal for the Communities £50 million (2001–2011)
- URBAN 2 £16 million (2000–2006)[1]

Regeneration measures have been implemented with the best intentions, stressing the importance of 'partnership, sustainability, people focus, work as a route out of poverty, connectivity, opportunity and influence'. As the local authority and, not least, deprived communities have come to recognize, however, the social impact of regeneration schemes has been uneven and not everyone has benefited.

As the regeneration literature provided by the council notes, a considerable slice of the regeneration pie has been spent on improving the environment through physical regeneration projects, including substantial investment in retail and the cultural industries in areas within Lambeth, such as Brixton, as we saw earlier. To an extent the regeneration programme has worked to make a once-notorious inner-city area attractive both to business and to new professionals who have moved into what is recognized as an increasingly desirable place to live. The 'success' attendant upon building a successful and dynamic 24-hour night-time economy, however, comes with significant issues attached. The renaissance has brought into the area the kind of population which now constitutes the majority of the victim population. As new (predominantly white) professionals have arrived, they have also pushed up land and property prices. These are now well beyond the reach of poor populations, who are left with no alternative but to occupy areas characterized by highly deprived and physically denuded estates. Neither has the regeneration effort offset the pattern of existing deprivation in the area to a significant extent, or at least to an extent to which it might impact on rates of crime. Nor has it compensated for economic changes that still act to produce a highly inequitable distribution of life chances in the area.

The facts are stark. As regeneration literature provided by Lambeth Council shows, it is the only borough in central London 'to have experienced a net loss of employment over the period 1991–1998'. The report also states that the area has 'the highest number of unemployed claimants in the central London area across all age groups and for all durations'. Though unemployment and deprivation remains a factor impacting negatively on the health and wellbeing of all ethnic communities in the borough, its impact has been experienced acutely by the area's indigenous black population, which unsurprisingly makes up the vast majority of street crime offenders.

Let us now draw together the unintended consequences of regeneration policy. By making Lambeth more attractive to professionals and businesses, while doing little to improve the conditions of deprivation experienced by local communities, the cumulative and unintended effect has been to accentuate relative deprivation as opposed to reducing it. As a strategy that might be expected to improve the social conditions that provoke criminal adaptations, the net effect has been to accentuate the very conditions that provoke it. Hell, as they say, is often built on the best of intentions.

The coordination and integration of community safety

Let me now conclude this analysis of control effort by examining issues pertinent to its coordination and integration. In the era of holistic, joined-up policy and sustained multiagency working, just how holistic and joined-up has community safety effort proved to be? As I will now argue in the case of street robbery in Lambeth, an important and contributing factor to its increase was certainly the failure to have in place a co-ordinated and well-organized community safety strategy.

At first sight, the borough may be considered to have met most of the terms of the 1998 Crime and Disorder Act in the organization of its community safety effort. It has a crime unit attached to the local authority, it has constructed a Youth Offending Team and has formalized multi-agency partnership working through the creation of a Crime and Disorder Executive and Community Safety Partnership. It also has a dedicated series of working groups in the field of community safety, not least among which is a street crime strategy group.

If we consider how this control system operated and focused its effort on confronting street crime, a number of issues can be raised regarding its effectiveness. Cumulatively, as we shall see, the various bodies act to subvert the aim of confronting street crime in an effective and concerted way.

First, while multiagency working was a feature of the borough, not all relevant agencies were represented. Education and Youth Services tended to avoid contact with community safety providers, even though both might well be regarded as being of fundamental importance in helping to develop policies to confront offences like street robbery. This absence could be considered a product of three factors. First, ignorance of the implications of section 17 of the Crime and Disorder Act meant that many key authorities did not believe that crime was anything to do with them at all. This was certainly the case with local schools. Second, most parts of the local council operated under the illusion that the council's crime-reduction role was solely the responsibility of its appallingly under-funded Crime Unit. Third – and importantly – the autonomy conceded to local schools in order to 'free' them from local authority control meant that they had no obligation to become involved in collective efforts to confront crime. Many, it could be observed, decided not to. Nor for that matter did local political elites who, in the face of rising crime figures, appeared unwilling to associate themselves with community safety providers in a context where efforts to confront street crime did not appear to be working. In fact, political elites in the area had until 2002 favoured maintaining a complete distance from law-enforcement agencies altogether. Practically, this resolved itself in non-attendance at multiagency partnership boards and, in the case of the then ruling party (a New Labour administration), a consistent unwillingness to meet with the Metropolitan Police commander, even when this was requested. Local politics and crime were therefore never meaningfully connected in Lambeth, even though high rates of street crime in the borough were perceived both locally and nationally as a serious issue. When finally the New Labour administration did get around to addressing the scale of the problem (after visits from Home office ministers and not least the reality check posed by local elections), their intervention was less than impressive. Despite being a nominally left-of-centre administration, they had no hesitation in adopting a hard-line punitive strategy. If elected they claimed they would create a 'multi-agency zero-tolerance hit squad'. They were not re-elected.

Though community safety is a term often used in criminological literature to describe local crime effort, in many respects if the term is used to define a holistic approach to the problems posed by street crime, it is hard to suggest that this can be observed in practice. Government-established priorities have typically focused on situational prevention, not least through the provision of significant sums of money that local authorities are then obligated to bid for (Hughes 2002). As for more proactive measures then, as we have seen above, those who might be expected to be involved in these either absent themselves from the policy-making table, or are so autonomous that they are not obligated to sit at the table at all. The sheer proliferation of funding streams and the orientation towards short-term funding also subverts ideas of collective effort or effort that works towards securing long-term goals. The number of strings typically attached to projects funded by government, working as they do in conjunction with systemic biases that favour situational prevention, also prevent a wider and more holistic agenda being pursued, because the necessary autonomy local partnerships require to plan in this way is effectively subverted. What these constraints result in, I would suggest, is the construction of a climate in which developing a fully holistic and comprehensive solution to street robbery is always likely to be subverted from the beginning. This has certainly been the case in Lambeth, as its rising robbery rate suggests.

The inherent disorganization in community safety practice itself fuels this fragmentation, not least because it provokes the development of more managerialist solutions to wider social problems that are then imposed by government to ensure more joined-up thinking, better partnership working, etc. in a policy context that already subverts such outcomes to begin with. Lambeth was an interesting case study into the nature and often futility of such measures. Let me explain.

In the face of the street robbery epidemic in Lambeth, the government (after seeking to blame everyone else for the problem) decided to initiate firm action. Deputations of the powerful were despatched to Lambeth with orders to 'knock heads together',[2] while advisory bodies such as Government Office for London (itself under pressure from the government) unleashed a stream of managerial directives designed to integrate and coordinate community safety effort more effectively. At its best this pressure would eventually lead to a more integrated structure of provision within the borough. It would certainly lead the council to place crime control far more at the centre of its agenda than had hitherto been the case. Managerialism, however, has its limits and any consideration of deficits in control has to address these.

The chosen vehicle by which the government and its advisors chose to improve the system of delivery in Lambeth (as well as other high street crime boroughs) lay in making local crime-prevention teams develop a barrage of strategies designed to address the problem. Many of these involved serious duplication with other strategies. Thus, in addition to having to deliver a Crime and Disorder Audit along with an associated

Local Crime Reduction Strategy (in line with statutory responsibilities under the terms of the 1998 Crime and Disorder Act), 'high crime' boroughs such as Lambeth were also obligated to produce Youth Crime Reduction Strategies as well. These required the production of action plans and were, not least, supposed to link directly with the wider crime-reduction strategy. Without even pausing to consider whether or not the wider strategy already contained a street crime reduction element (it did), under government pressure inner-city London boroughs were directed to prepare a street crime reduction strategy as well as and in addition to the others.

Only this time, things were going to be different. For far from a strategy giving rise to an action plan – with a panoply of bench marks and milestones so favoured by British society – the government instructed local crime-prevention boards to reverse the process and produce their action plans *before* the strategy. Yes, before the strategy itself had been formulated, and therefore a procedure that eliminated any rationality that actually remained in the system to begin with. Needless to say, this all required a considerable effort, and was also exacerbated by the injunction on local partnerships to forward the results of all initiatives that might have a bearing on street robbery on an ongoing monthly basis in order to demonstrate how successful the initiatives were.

While this might appear to have been a serious attempt to make errant crime-reduction teams responsible at the local level, as someone working in the policy field this was not how it appeared to me (I was working at that time as an advisor to the community safety partnership). What was really going on was far less rational behaviour that made a difference, and far more an exercise in symbolic governance (this could also be read as a serious disconfirmation of Garland's thesis about the inherent rationality of what he positively terms 'the criminologies of everyday life' (Garland 1996).) What it involved was the production of vast quantities of paper that reconstructed the real world in a simulation that bore little relation to reality. It was all profoundly postmodern.

Though the barrage of government initiatives made little sense from the standpoint of practical intervention, as Tonry has convincingly argued, in many respects it was not the audience of practitioners the government was seeking to appease. The real target, he suggests, was tabloid opinion, and this New Labour sought to manipulate through promoting symbolic initiatives designed to maintain the image of a hard-line law-and-order government getting to grips with serious problems. A strategy less evidence-based in its approach to the problem of street robbery and more 'improvisational', to use Tonry's term:

Astonishingly at a time when both official police data and the British Crime Survey's victimisation data showed overall crimes rates were declining, the government, the judiciary, and the Metropolitan Police panicked. In January 2002 the Court of Appeal in an opinion of Lord Justice Woolf held that a minimum 18-month prison sentence was appropriate for street robbers 'irrespective of the age of the offender' [...] In February the Metropolitan Police diverted hundreds of officers from other duties to focus on street crime in eight London boroughs. Also in February Tony Blair established a street crime committee and assigned 10 ministers to oversee street crime initiatives in ten areas. In March Blair convened the first of a series of multi agency meetings in Downing Street and Blunkett initiated his Street Crime initiative in which 5,000 officers were diverted from other issues. (Tonry 2004)

Conclusion

In conclusion, while the rise of street robbery can certainly be attributed to the problems posed by motivated offenders targeting suitable and available targets, this is only part of the problem. As this chapter has tried to demonstrate, any consideration of rising street robbery must also look at the deficits in social control that rising street robbery clearly demonstrates. As this chapter has established, rising robbery, not least in high-crime areas such as Lambeth, was provoked by failures in the way the problem was policed and offenders dealt with, by inappropriate social interventions, and the irrational application of situational crime prevention measures.

Notes

1 Source: Lambeth Regeneration and Planning Department (unpublished report 2002).
2 On two occasions during the period of research I conducted in Lambeth, I heard the borough described in these terms by various Home Office officials.

Chapter 10

Conclusion

Having produced a book on street robbery, it would now appear incumbent to conclude by providing some answers to the question, 'What is to be done to prevent it?' This, after all, would provide a neat closure around the issues I have been discussing, and would chime well with the general ethos of administrative criminology which stresses the need to develop pragmatic solutions to the problems posed by crime.

While recognizing that providing suitable solutions is what I am supposed to be in the business of doing, I nevertheless feel obliged to refuse the invitation – at least at this moment. This is not, I hasten to add, because I am of the opinion that we should do nothing, or that suggestions concerning what should be done about street crime are none of my business. My problem is that I remain unconvinced that the ways we have been enjoined to consider street robbery and intervene to prevent it are ultimately the right ways. To begin with, I remain deeply troubled by the interpretative grid that has been applied to make sense of street robbery. As a society we are not, I would say, looking at the problem in the right way. The second problem follows on from this, for if our explanations err, then so do the policies posed as solutions. For just as night follows day, so the one follows from the other. To put this another way, if there are problems in our interpretation, there will be problems in the solutions that we select on the basis of it. This is, at the same time, a normative problem as well as a question of what works and what does not. It is normative precisely because the solutions we apply might not only fail, but they may also be profoundly unjust at the point of implementation. The problem of crime, after all, is as much a problem of control as it is of people breaking rules.

Therefore, before we get to the part where questions about 'What is to be done?' are resolved into a package of neat and tidy prescriptions, we need to reconsider the way in which we have been enjoined to think about street crime. For unless we see the world aright, we run the risk of compounding one series of mistakes with others. With this injunction in mind, I will present a critique of what I consider the orthodoxy on street crime. I will then reconsider on the basis of this an alternative reading predicated upon the analysis I have developed. I will conclude by offering a few suggestions that follow from my prognosis.

So where are we going wrong? To answer this question, we need to re-examine what passes for the dominant orthodoxy on street crime. For while, as we saw earlier, there may well be a rich tapestry of explanations for street robbery, it is worth bearing in mind that not all are accorded an equal status in the life of society. Some come to achieve prominence and are accorded the status of 'truth', and, on the basis of these, policy decisions are made. Unfortunately the criteria of evidence and the application of common sense count for little in deciding which inter-pretations prevail, as we shall now observe.

Perhaps the most axiomatic and seemingly self-evident truth upon which the emerging orthodoxy on street robbery is premised is the pervasive assumption that street robbery is not a problem of *our* society, so much as a problem that emanates from outside, whatever we imagine this 'outside' to be. There is, or so this narrative imagines, an entity called society that is essentially good. It is a place full of decent, hard-working people doing enterprising things. Unfortunately, their capacity to do this in recent years has been curtailed as a consequence of rising crime. It comes in many forms and street robbery represents one of its worst expressions. As the state has not put in place the measures necessary to confront street robbery, so the problem has escalated – or so it is asserted. The good society has consequently been transformed into a society of victims.

The source of this problem is typically identified (as we have seen) with a criminal class conceived in terms that define them as para-digmatic outsiders. These are the street robbers: a population composed of strangers who are strange precisely because they are alien. This alien quality is attested to again and again through a criminology of 'essentualised difference' through which their outsider status is both defined and confirmed (Garland 1996). These are folk devils whose devil status is exemplified by their socio-economic position (as underclass); by their familial status (the mal-socialized offspring of feckless mothers); by their race (read 'black mugger'); and by the deviant behaviour in which they engage (the use of illegal drugs and their love affair with casual undiscriminating violence).

My point is this. If we begin with this interpretation and apply it to make sense of the problem of street robbery, it is easy to see how a certain array of solutions follows through from the prognosis it offers. For if the problem to the inside (the good society) is that posed to it by a lawless predatory outside (the underclass), then self-evidently the policy response must be to defend the good society from its outside. So a particular set of 'solutions' follows logically through from the prognosis offered. One would include intensifying the defences of the good society in order better to protect it from the enemy it confronts. Another would be to heighten its vigilance in order better to know what its outside is doing. These represent the kind of proactive measures that could be put in place. There are, needless to say, more reactive responses. These typically coalesce around the metaphor of a war. These would include taking the appropriate steps to ensure that the outside is beaten back; or alternatively, is taken out of circulation in ways that prevent its lethal contagion. If this sounds too simple, let us consider just how far this prognosis logically predicts the kinds of solutions we have seen actively posed and proposed to the problem of street crime in recent years.

For intensifying defences read the gated community, situational crime prevention and what Davis has identified as the pervasive 'militarisation' of public space that has followed through in its wake (Davis 1990). For heightened vigilance read pervasive surveillance evident in the rise of CCTV. As for 'beating back' the threat, read zero-tolerance policing and increasing levels of stop-and-search directed at the young and, not least, black communities. As for policies that embody the need to remove the 'outsider' from circulation, read longer prison sentences, the renaissance of incapacitation and – as an inevitable outcome – the highest prison population in postwar British history.

The move from definition to solutions conceived in these terms appears entirely logical and, to many, entirely just. After all, if the street robber is an alien, and a dangerous one at that, then clearly all the policy options outlined above must make good sense. Not only are they workable solutions, but they are, in terms of this line of reasoning, also socially just in that 'just deserts' are seen to be delivered to those for whom harsh punishment is no more than deserved. Given the punitive nature of our times, these policies also appear to chime well with the needs of law and order that the public appears to demand from its populist and authoritarian New Labour government.

My problem with this interpretation is that I do not accept the prognosis offered and remain deeply concerned about the array of policies that are touted as its 'logical' solution. I oppose the prognosis on the basis that, far from being an accurate representation of the truth of street crime, it presents an untruth. As I will argue, street robbery, far from being a problem society faces, is on the contrary a problem *of* our society and of its contemporary organization and structure. The robber is not an independent variable, but a dependent one. Just as I hold the interpretation of the problem to be suspect, so I also remain deeply worried about the kind of solutions that have been proposed to address it, as these are shaped within and by this interpretation. My worries here not only relate to the fact that many of the solutions are inappropriate and consequently will not accomplish what is expected of them, but also that they fail because it is my contention they are unjust. Finally, I remain opposed to this orthodoxy because in its hegemony it reinforces a kind of common sense about crime that is dangerous. In particular, it reinforces the illusion that crime is associated with the most marginal sections of our society, while absolving society and the powerful from their role in creating the preconditions in which street crime flourishes.

When I argue that we need to conceive the problem of street robbery as a problem of our society, my aim is to challenge the view that follows from the dominant orthodoxy, which – as we have seen – is to consider the robber as an outsider. Against this interpretative orthodoxy, I want to restate the case for a *criminology of sameness* not of *essentualized difference*, a criminology that recognizes the street robber as product of our society and of the way in which our free-market capitalist society is organized. In so doing, I want to suggest that the issue I am addressing is not a minor squabble over semantics. On the contrary, it is fundamental to how we perceive and ultimately engage with the problems street robbery poses.

My disagreement with those who believe that the street robber is an alien outsider are developed in Chapter 4, which examined and criticized the forms of underclass thinking upon which this interpretation rests. The terms of my critique were to suggest, in opposition to such approaches, that they systematically overstated the otherness of the street robber while losing sight of the many characteristics that unified this figure with the society that had in effect produced him as a folk devil. Most street robbers, as we saw, possessed moral consciousness, most did not conceive their future in terms of a criminal career, and none of them was driven to street robbery by the demands of a chaotic drug culture.

More to the point, as my own research confirmed, to understand why they came to street robbery it was profoundly important to recognize how far their need to possess the consumer objects they sought to appropriate was a function of free-market capitalism and the cult of compulsory consumption around which it is organized. Far from being, as underclass thinking would categorize them, mal-socialized individuals, my research leads me to the conclusion that they are in fact dangerously over-socialized, as their socialization is shaped by their all-too-successful induction to capitalist consumption norms. To put the matter bluntly, the street robbery problem in its contemporary form is a problem of a society that induces young people to desire and covet the very goods they have been pressurized from an early age to associate with the good life. The kind of designer branded objects, in other words, they have been led to desire through their exposure to the capitalist culture industries that target them remorselessly and relentlessly. At the same time, as we have also seen, this is a society which, while inducing a universal desire on the part of young people to build their lifestyles and establish their identifies through consumption, does not equip everyone with the wherewithal to consume legitimately. Street robbers, while very successful consumers, are nevertheless flawed consumers, and that is their and our problem.

If this is the case, blaming young people for doing what they have been led to understand is essential to their lives – that is, to consume often and always – is a mistaken strategy, even if it is convenient. After all, we have created the preconditions for the crime in which a growing number of young people have become engaged. We have programmed them to consume voraciously, to consume in order to manufacture their designer brand lifestyles, and we are then surprised when they perform in accordance with the given programme.

This is not, I recognize, a proposition many would like to countenance. After all, maintaining the image of the street robber as outsider is morally convenient. More than that, it makes for good denial. Besides, if we do proceed on the basis that the robber is one of us and a product of the social arrangements that define our society, then this line of reasoning starts to raise a number of unpleasant implications for the kind of society we have established for the young.

But the way the free-market society is organized is precisely the problem, and we need to address it head-on if we are both to make sense of street crime and consider what and how we should respond to it. Might it be that the problem we are dealing with here is very much a problem of a society which in its nature is inhuman and which ultimately dehumanizes those subject to its fatal embrace? Might the street robber be as much a victim of the free market as he is an offender that mercilessly targets its citizens?

To examine this hypothesis, let us return once again to the facts: young people who consume in order to construct their identities; who will even risk serious punishment if legitimate consumption routes are blocked; and who will victimize those whose consumption is not deemed to be appropriate.

My point is this. While it is easy to demonize the street criminal for their inhumanity, these strange behavioural rituals are entirely consistent with the seductive and spectacular world that consumer capitalism has built and to which these young people have been so relentlessly exposed. They are not, I am suggesting, acting against the flow of the desires it wishes to marshal and harness in pursuit of its profit; on the contrary, they are perfect desiring machines reproduced exactly in its image, forged in the furnace of its being. They want what it requires them to want – the goods produced by the culture industries. They want this so badly that they cannot visualize life without such things because – and this is where the machine is all-too-successful – out of these ephemeral objects their life is established and their identities constructed. Out of it, as we have seen, their habitat is established and, through the rituals of possession and non-possession, distinction achieved or denied.

It is of course an impressive achievement to have produced desiring beings in this image. Brilliant really. Such a depth of penetration can only be visualized as an index of the sophistication of the capitalist juggernaut itself. It really is tantamount to what Jameson identified many years ago as the cultural industry's full and complete commodification of the lifeworld and its penetration of the unconscious (Jameson 1984). Healthy and productive however it certainly is not. In my estimation, the logic of compulsory consumption is at least as unhealthy as the violence that street robbers use to appropriate the goods they have been socialized through it to desire and covet. And this is the rub. Without the one we would not be confronting the other. Before we direct our vengeance at the robbers for the impertinence of their flawed consumption, let us be quite clear about the nature of the culture industry that helped produce them as consumers. As Adorno and Horkhiemer wrote many years ago:

> The culture industry perpetually cheats its consumers of what it permanently promises. The promissory note which, with its plots and staging, it draws on pleasure is endlessly prolonged, the promise, which is all the spectacle consists of, is illusory: all it actually confirms is that the real point will not be reached, that the diner must be satisfied with the menu. (Horkhiemer and Adorno 1973)

Capitalism may claim to offer everything to everyone, but what it really offers in its free-market form is an impoverished world that impoverishes the individuals within it. In the manner of a vacuum, it also removes the oxygen in which other alternatives might thrive. Alternatives that might place limits on consumption by suggesting a vision of the good life as something beyond or outside of the desire to consume relentlessly. The problem of our age, though, is that commodification is everything and everywhere. In the final analysis, it is all that there is.

As we saw when we considered the world of the offender, outside the pull of the peer group and the commodified culture out of which it produced itself, there really was little else available to these young men as an alternative. Jobs for life were no longer part of what growing up meant, because the offenders grew up in a post-full employment society. They really were disadvantaged, as this process also blocked the transition to adulthood that full-time work had once historically conceded to working-class men. As for religion, it meant nothing to them. And politicians? These were simply distant, irrelevant and distrusted. Politics as such meant nothing. As for role models – they simply had none.

They inhabited, in other words, a world where free-market capitalism had won out over everything else. This really was a world which had achieved the 'end of history' (Rukeyama 1992). A world where rampant free-market capitalism was everything and where the mark of the market was all there was. While their abandonment of emancipatory politics might well be placed at the door of young people's disenchantment with the mendacity of politicians today, as well as the failure of faith communities to speak to them in terms to which they can relate, such an interpretation is nevertheless flawed. What it overlooks is just how successful capitalism in its free-market form has been in eliminating from the world any alternative to it. Seabrook draws out well the implications of this hyper-real world and its impact on young people. 'To grow up under the domination of consumer capitalism is', he argues:

> to see that part of us which used to belong to society to be colonised, torn away from traditional allegiances, and to be hurtled, alone and isolated into the prison of an individual's senses. The child tends to be stripped of all social influences but that of the market-place; all sense of place, function and class are weakened; the characteristics of region or clan, neighbourhood or kindred are attenuated. The individual is denuded of everything but appetites, desires and tastes, wrenched from any context of human obligation

or commitment. It is a process of mutilation; and once this has been achieved we are offered the consolation of reconstructing the abbreviated humanity out of the things and the goods around us, and the fantasies and vapours which they emit. (Seabrook 1978)

This is a good description of the world the street robber inhabits. Their 'mutilated' world, and ours as well. The inhumanity of free-market capitalism is that its way of being sets in motion the logic of consumption that establishes the basis for the consuming desire that underpins the contemporary problem of street crime. As we have also seen, its commodifying logic has helped to eliminate alternatives that might negate this desire.

What really separates the street robber from young people in general, however, is not the will to consume or the dominance of consumption rites in their life. All young people, it could be argued, are subject to and subjugated by this consuming imperative. What really separates them is access to those avenues where consumption can be gratified legitimately. At the end of the day, it is their subjugation to consumption *in addition* to being situated in a socio-economic context where consumption rites can not be legitimately satisfied that provokes the Mertonian adaptation that resolves itself into street robbery. In other words, by consumption pursued through illegal means. If the free market has subjugated young street robbers at the point of their desire, it also excludes them forcefully from those avenues that might allow consumption desires to be sublimated legitimately. As it incorporates them in one way, so it systematically excludes them in others.

Jock Young has recently and powerfully drawn attention to this strange kind of society (Young 2001), a society that simultaneously expels the very beings it incorporates in other ways. His powerful metaphor is that of bulimia and the bulimic society. This condition, he argues, is not simply a pathology of young women whose lives revolve around rituals characterized by eating and vomiting. This trait also describes well the operation of the contemporary free-market society. On the one hand, it opens its arms to all, promising a future of eternal material bliss. On the other, its social relations systematically ensure that many are excluded from this material dream by being denied the opportunity through which it can be appropriated.

The street robbers I studied in Lambeth illustrate this contradiction starkly in their lives. They want and desire the good life as it is pre-packaged in its commodified form by the culture industries. They want to move onwards and outwards; they can visualize exit strategies. At the same time this life is not achievable within the terms of the class position they have been allocated, in the very areas where they are forced to grow up.

It is this feature of late capitalism, its pathological bulimic quality, that distinguishes it from its earlier incarnation. And it is this feature that makes the kind of street robbery we see in areas such as Lambeth today different from that which prevailed in earlier times. In earlier phases of its development, capitalism simply produced a class which was totally excluded. This is the class of poor people studied by people like Mayhew. In such an exclusionary order, robbery was not conditioned by the need to construct an elaborate lifestyle, but emerged as a pragmatic response to terrible patterns of deprivation and poverty. For those with nothing, it really did mark a survival choice. What you appropriated could be exchanged for the bare necessities of life. It could be observed that this is a perennial feature of poor societies. It is and remains a source of livelihood for those who have none.

While certainly located in poorer socio-economic groups, the street robbers of today are different because they rob not in order to provide the means for survival but to construct through the appropriation of desirable goods a lifestyle and through this an identity they conceive as essential to their wellbeing. To look at this another way, you do not need to steal mobile phones in order to eat, you do so in order to accumulate the appropriate symbolic capital through which being – as it is defined within consumer capitalism – is accorded meaning. Yes it is still about questions of survival, but the terms by which survival is now registered have changed significantly.

At this point, let me attempt to offset a criticism I can sense being directed at this kind of analysis. This would be to suggest that I am presenting the street robber as someone who in effect does not make choices. My analysis, it could be claimed, denies their humanity even in my attempt to restate it. It does so by presenting an over-socialized view of the subject. In terms of this critique, I could be considered to have produced a vision of an individual who has no capacity to exercise free will, and who is simply a product of forces acting over and beyond them.

My response to this would be to return to the analysis I offered in earlier chapters which, while attempting to understand what might be considered the deeper structuring forces that propel young people to crime, also examined processes of differential association as these were also experienced. As this analysis made clear, the route-way towards crime was by no means simple. Choices could be made. There was no one-way street. The making of choices, however, was always, as I also sought to establish, initiated within parameters established by the nature of the world in which they lived and the round of their lives. These were, from the outset, also curtailed in terms of the possibilities they made available or obviated. A particular configuration of forces, for example, could well make the road to street crime a likely choice for a particular young man, especially when this configuration involves finding yourself in the proximity of already existing outlaw cultures, a highly developed illegal and grey market, and a general cultural tolerance of street crime among your peer group. It could well be, though, that even in the context of such a world the choice to commit crime was not made. Maybe some significant person could and did make a difference. Nothing, in other words, is inevitable. Most young people, after all, do not go on to become street criminals.

Having reconsidered the way we have often been enjoined to examine street crime, I now feel at last able to conclude with some final thoughts on what should be done about the problems street robbery poses. There are, of course, a number of ways in which this game could be played out. Before offering my final thoughts on the matter, let me briefly review the solution society has unfortunately elected. As we saw above, this involved seeking to raise society's defences against the outsider, allied to a more punitive thrust directed at waging war with them.

Now I recognize that this is certainly a popular move in the kind of law-and-order society we unfortunately inhabit. I also recognize that by increasing the net capacity of the repressive apparatus, at a certain point in time it might well pay some dividends. This of course presupposes that rates of detection dramatically improve, that blockages in the judicial process are removed (which would lower attrition rates), and that the government shows willing to incarcerate even more young men. This is certainly the solution favoured by the right, and to its ongoing detriment appears to be the solution appropriated by the New Labour government of Blair and Blunkett. Integral to the way in which this vision of success was presented was a call upon the government to embrace US-style zero-tolerance policies. Before we embrace US-style mass incarceration, however, and before we subject our police to yet further paramilitarization, we need to be mindful of a few truths about what is being proposed.

To accomplish this, let us consider in turn the idea that we can (a) police our way out of street crime; (b) design our way out of it; and (c) lock our way out of it. While zero tolerance might well be the preferred option of many, it is worth noting that the aggressive targeting of young men in poor areas is by no means new. On the contrary, this is very much the kind of policing that black communities in areas such as Brixton were already subject to in the not-too-distant past (Scarman

1981). As it was then and as it is now, such a policy is likely to provoke a backlash far worse than the problems it wishes to solve, particularly given that large numbers of innocent young people are likely to be on the receiving end of the repression at the core of the 'solution'. It was in recognition of this that the police division in Lambeth sensibly avoided a zero-tolerance approach more recently in its own more measured approach to street robbery. Just as importantly, while the tabloid right unquestioningly accepts that zero tolerance actively reduces crime, more detailed and sober analysis of the evidence by no means supports such a claim (Bowling 1999).

The blanket and undiscriminating side of other repressive legislation pioneered by New Labour in recent years, such as curfew and anti-social behaviour orders, also falls foul of a similar critique. It might appease the right and might also send out the right electoral signal to a security-conscious and insecure public, but at the point of implementation, such policies are destined to failure. In and of themselves they will not stop or terminate street robbery. They remain simply unworkable aspects of symbolic governance in the context of a society that has well and truly lost its way on law and order.

Locking our way out of the street crime problem remains, as we have seen, another popular solution in the authoritarian armoury. It clearly remains a popular project, but is one fraught, I would suggest, with numerous risks and dangers attached. These ultimately undermine its credibility as either an appropriate response or indeed a just one. As a solution it entails embracing the idea that prison actually works as a disincentive to offenders and thus constitutes an appropriate response to the problem street robbery poses. These assumptions, however, do not stand up to critical scrutiny, as we shall now see.

Let us begin with the question of whether or not prison actually works. The first response to this would be to suggest that there is little evidence to show that rehabilitation is what prison achieves, even if this is its stated purpose. As my interviews with young offenders suggested, the judicial ritual was not one they had much respect for, nor indeed is it designed in ways that lead people to respect it. The language of law was impenetrable to them, while the judiciary were simply considered as figures of oppression that had very little to do with justice. While it cannot be denied that some offenders came to see the error of their ways, once subject to the dehumanizing regimes of prison life many more clearly did not. In fact, research suggests a 'revolving door' system often operates. According to the government's own figures around 60 per cent of offenders are destined to leave prison and offend again. Prison, despite our endless investment in it, does not work to make bad people better. All it typically does is brutalize better those who have already been brutalized.

Given that the majority of street robbers are under 18, it could be remarked that if Lord Woolf's call to imprison these was taken at face value, the government would not only be pushing more young people into precisely the kind of places they need to avoid, but it would also mean abandoning one of the few government initiatives that was actually evidence-based. This was the truth, stated clearly in the 1998 Crime and Disorder Act, that held that locking young people away was ultimately a counterproductive thing to do and consequently needed to be avoided where possible. This truth was embraced in the creation of Youth Offending Teams which had as their mission a clear commitment to ensure that under-18s were dealt with through non-punitive measures where at all possible. Promoting Orwellian double-think is of course something all governments engage in, not least in pursuit of demonstrating effective statecraft to their sceptical electorates. Quite why New Labour should choose to abandon one of the few intelligent planks of its penal policy, however, beggars belief. What it does suggest is just how cravenly abject the government can be to the right-wing tabloids and their distorted perspectives on law and order (Tonry 2004).

Next there is the vexed question of whether or not a prison sentence is a just punishment for street robbery. Now clearly if a person is assaulted and if serious injuries are sustained, then a good case could be made for such a sentence. As our research in Lambeth indicated, however, a prison sentence, far from being used as a means of last resort for the worst street crime offenders, had become the single preferred way of addressing the problem, specifically for those over the age of 18. Indeed, as the figures graphically indicate, if you were black you would invariably receive a prison sentence, even if the offence was your first (Hallsworth and Richie 2002). Indeed, a sentence of incarceration for street robbery in Lambeth was far more likely than the possibility of receiving one for assault. This might well be read as indicative of the success of a project built on a politics of judicial vengeance, but from where I stand it appears symptomatic of a sense of reason that has gone astray.

The adherents of lock-down solutions might do well to consider the material cost of the incarceration policies they want to sanction. A mobile phone costs around £100. It costs over £35,000 per year to imprison an offender for stealing one. There is no reason to suppose that a single prison sentence will be the last for those sent to prison the first time round. Incarceration is not, in other words, value for money or money well spent. If private corporations operated the same way, they would undeniably be closed down.

Finally, let us consider the implications that follow though from that other great growth industry, situational crime prevention. Is it possible to solve the problem of street crime by aspiring simply to design the problem away? Though I remain sceptical of situational approaches, not least because these are too often disarticulated from a social crime-prevention agenda, there is certainly a case to be made for suggesting that this approach offers a better chance of success than the repressive measures considered above. Having made this point, it must be noted that the success of an intervention strategy is measured not by what it may promise but by what it concretely achieves. Despite all its talk of identifying 'rational' and 'pragmatic' solutions to problems such as street robbery, and despite the huge sums of money invested in implementing such solutions in relation to it, situational crime prevention has failed spectacularly.

As I argued in Chapter 9, the kinds of situational defences that could have worked were never implemented, for example immobilizing mobile phones after they had been stolen. At the same time, expensive interventions that did not work were implemented with a recklessness that was extraordinary. And so we find ourselves today inhabiting a country subject to more pervasive CCTV than any other society in the world – without any tangible evidence that this technology could and does prevent street robbery. As with zero-tolerance policing and other reflex strategies such as curfew, what this particular instance of 'pragmatic' what-works criminology represents is less a rational 'joined-up' response to a particular problem and far more a symbolic, politically motivated empty gesture with sinister overtones.

So what can be done to confront street robbery? I will begin by presenting the less contentious of my conclusions. I will finish by presenting some ideas many are likely to find less acceptable. All, as we shall see, follow through from my reading of the problem of street robbery less as an independent variable and more as a dependent variable, and thus as a product of our society.

While we must always accept street robbers as a product of the kind of society in which we live, this does not mean that things do not need to be done actively to prevent them from perpetrating more robbery. Free-market capitalism is a brutalizing force, but this does not obviate or excuse the brutality of street robbery. Clearly those who engage in it need to be stopped.

To stop them, however, we need to engage with solutions that do not dissolve into a destructive war premised upon a politics of judicial vengeance. To begin with, we do not require in any shape or form the kind of reactive zero-tolerance policing the tabloid right want to see imposed. Nor do we require a further intensification of ill-thought-out unworkable blanket strategies such as curfews. Finally, and this is perhaps the single most important intervention initiative I can suggest, we do not require symbolic kneejerk political interventions designed to play to the court of tabloid reactionary opinion. Effective solutions require, on the contrary, implementing proportionate intelligence-led approaches to the problem, and this is somewhat different. In fact, it means doing precisely what the police have begun to initiate anyway in schemes such as Safer Streets, which develop new ways of responding to the problem of street crime where it occurs. As they have found, this might mean placing extra police in street crime hot spots, using and developing better intelligence, and responding faster to crimes when they have been perpetrated. Such an approach does not preclude robust policing, but it does delimit how it is deployed and to whom.

Though I have been critical of the way situational crime prevention has or indeed has not been used to confront street robbery, this does not also mean it cannot play an important role in the solution to the problems street robbery poses. There is indeed a lot that can be accomplished. Most significantly, though entirely belatedly, most phone companies have now bitten the bullet and have finally introduced the means necessary to immobilize mobile phones. It should have been forced upon them far earlier, but better late than never. Design solutions to street robbery, however, do not stop at the level of the mobile phone. The way that bags are designed is also significant. You cannot, for example, grab a rucksack in the same way as you can a handbag, and potential victims need better education in order to ensure that they remain aware of common-sense solutions such as this. On a positive note, victim education is now recognized as an important variable by crime prevention partnerships, even if it will only ever reap limited dividends.

It will by now have become evident that I am no lover of our prison system or of the control agents that manage it. Pushing young men through it constitutes, as I have argued above, a costly mistake. It will not stop crime, it is a prohibitively expensive option and it does little to confront offending behaviour among its client group. The real winners of this particular lottery are those who always win anyway – the professionals that thrive on crime and the harvest it reaps for them assessed in terms of the material rewards they claim.

With this in mind, all I can do is remind the government of what its sensible advisors have already argued: do not imprison more, imprison less; and more than that, find better alternatives to prison as a matter of urgency. Though it remains a solution that has yet to prove itself, the decision to establish Youth Offending Teams was by and large a good idea, as was the decision to use them as vehicles through which to process young people under 18 as an alternative to gaol. If I have two recommendations to make, the first is that it is not just the under-18s who need saving from the judges and a prison sentence. Many young people who are older than this arbitrary cut-off point also need to be dealt with in a similar way, and this is something that needs to be addressed urgently. Secondly, if street robbery has social causes, do not believe its solution can be found in subjugating the offender to courses in ill-placed and ill-thought-out cognitive therapy. The street crime problem is with society, not within the individual and his or her anger.

I am far more for a system of control that places the business of punishment back in the community. Having interviewed numerous offenders, what often struck me was how alienated they were from the people who typically tried them. Would it not, as a consequence, be far better, to subjugate these young people to those whose opinions they might just respect, rather than leave them to the world of magistrates and judges whose opinions they do not? The kinds of people, in other words, notoriously absent from our system of 'justice'. While this may be read as a support for restorative justice, this support is qualified. Using restorative justice methods such as Restitution Orders as yet another adjunct to the judicial response young people receive anyway appears to me to be less 'restorative' and far more a second punishment – not an alternative to the punishment they already receive. If we want to embed restorative justice it must be instead of judicial processing not simply another aspect of net-widening.

Using the police and the criminal justice system, though, is to deploy 'solutions' that are by their nature reactive, as opposed to proactive and preemptive. They invariably presuppose the horse has already bolted. Let me now conclude by considering what a proactive response might look like. That is, a response that addresses causes without seeking to devolve responsibility to the reactive forces that only deal with symptoms.

If there is to be a solution to street robbery, it must ultimately come through investing in the right way in poor communities. This must, though, mean thinking through how money is spent and what it is spent on. Lambeth, as we saw, like many other inner-city areas across the UK, had its social infrastructure literally torn out throughout the 1980s. While new money is certainly being pumped in through SRB, Communities Against Drugs and initiatives like Children's Fund, what must be recognized is that the overall funding is still woefully small and short-term in focus, even if headline figures look significant.[1] Projects for young people still remain terribly underfunded, while the kind of workers who might well make an important difference to young people and who work heroically with them (such as youth and community workers) have found their conditions of service ever more marginalized.

The problem is that while some good work to alleviate poverty within poor communities has been attempted, not enough has been done. Worse still, when social-regeneration initiatives are propounded as 'solutions', too often good work is compromised because the regeneration measure in question actually creates the preconditions for rising street robbery (as the example of Brixton's developing 24-hour night-time economy indicates), rather than attenuating them. The lesson for planners and policy makers is to think through far more clearly what the crime implications might be for the regeneration they plan. Lots of new bars in a 'poor' area, for example, might well raise the profile of the local economy, but can also create the preconditions for rising street robbery.

A further problem local communities face, as we have seen, is in securing the autonomy to implement solutions that are right for them. Too often, the funding available is only for what the government has already decided communities deserve, which is less 'government at a distance' so much as 'in your face'. Lambeth, as we saw, was a case study in twisted priorities. In 2002 it was awarded almost twice as much money from government to develop its CCTV surveillance than had been made available to fund its youth service. The solution to this problem is to let autonomy mean autonomy.

With this in mind may I offer my final solution. I regard it as a form of prudential reasoning and a form of risk management. Rather than put even more CCTV cameras into areas already awash with them, spend the money instead on youth services. Instead of sending young men to jails that fail, spend the money you will save on mobile phones and give these to young people. For one CCTV camera you can purchase a youth worker for a year. For the cost of one year's imprisonment, which now stands, according to Home Office figures for 2001, at £35,939 (Home Office 2003) two jobs could be created for young people without them, while almost 3,000 mobile phones could be purchased and distributed. A strange kind of economics to be sure, but then again this is a strange society to begin with. If practised, however, it could work.

Note

1   In 2004, the New Labour government announced significant cuts to Children's Fund, its 'flagship' youth regeneration programme.

Bibliography

Ackroyd, P. (2001) *London: The Biography*. London: Vintage.

Ainsworth, H. (1834) *Rookwood*. London: Richard Bentley.

Beggs, T. (1849) *An enquiry into the extent and causes of juvenile depravity*. London: Charles Gilpin.

Bellamy, J.G. (1964) 'The Coterel Gang: an Anatomy of a Band of Fourteenth-century Criminals', *English Historical Review*, 79: 698–717.

Blok, A. (2001) *Honour and Violence*. Cambridge: Polity Press.

Bowling, B. (1999) 'The Rise and Fall of New York Murder: Zero Tolerance or Crack's Decline?' *British Journal of Criminology*, 39 (4): 531–54.

Bowling, B. and Phillips, C. (2002) *Racism, Crime and Justice*. London: Longman.

Box, S. (1987) *Recession, Crime and Punishment*. Basingstoke: Macmillan.

Braithwaite, J. (1993) *Crime, Shame and Reintegration*. Cambridge: Cambridge University Press.

Briggs, J. (1996) *Crime and Punishment in England*. UCL Press.

Calender, N. (1779) *Newgate Calendar Vol. 1*. London: Alexander Hogg.

Cambell, B. (1993) *Goliath*. London: Methuen.

Caywood, T. (1998) 'Routine Activities and Urban Homicides: A tale of two cities', *Homicide Studies*, 2 (1): 64–82.

Clarke, R. (1980) 'Situational Crime Prevention: Theory and Practice', *British Journal of Criminology*, 20 (2): 136–47.

Clarke, R. and Meyhew, P. (eds) (1980) *Designing Out Crime*. London: HMSO.

Cohen, L.D.C. (1980) 'The determinants of larceny: An empirical and theoretical study', *Journal of Research in Crime and Delinquency*, 17: 140–90.

Cohen, L.E. and Felson, M. (1979) 'Social Trends and Crime Rate Trends: A Routine Activity Approach', *American Sociological Review*, 44: 588–607.

Cohen, S. (1980) *Folk Devils and Moral Panics*. London: Martin Robinson.

Cohen, S. (1981) Footprints in the Sand: A Further report on Criminology and the sociology of Deviance. *Crime and Society in Britain*. London: Routledge.

Cohen, S. (2001) *States of Denial*. Cambridge: Cambridge University Press.

Commission, H.M. (1888) *Calendar of the Manuscripts of the Marquis of Salisbury at Hatfield House, Part II*. London: HMSO.

Cote, J. and Allahar, A.L. (1996) *Generation on Hold: Coming of Age in the Late Twentieth Century*. London: New York University Press.

Croall, H. (1992) *White Collar Crime*. Buckingham: Open University Press.

Davis, J. (1980) 'The London Garotting Panic of 1862 and the Creation of a Criminal Class in Victorian England', in V. Gabrell, (ed.), *Crime and the Law: The Social History of Crime in Western Europe since 1500*. London: Europa.

Davis, M. (1990) *City of Quartz: Excavating the Future of Los Angles*. London: Verso.

Dickens, C. (1837–9 (1994)) *Oliver Twist*. London: Penguin Books.

Elias, N. (1978) *The Civilizing Process, Vol. 1: The History of Manners*. Oxford: Blackwell.

Engels, F. (1956) The Peasant War in Germany. *Marx-Engels, Selected Works, Vol. 2*. Moscow: Foreign Languages Publishing House.

Fidge, G. (1652) *The English Gusman*. London: James Hind.

Fielding, H. (1751 (1988)) *An enquiry into the causes of the late increases of robbers, and with some proposals for remedying this growing evil*, M. Zirkir (ed.), Midletown, Conneticut: Wesleyan University Press.

Fitzgerald, M.J.S. and Hale, C. (2002) *Young People and Street Crime*, Youth Justice Board.

Foucault, M. (1977) *Discipline and Punish, The Birth of the Prison*. London: Allen Lane.

Fukeyama, F. (1992) *The End of History and the Last Man*. New York: Free Press.

Garland, D. (1996) 'The Limits of the Sovereign State: Strategies of Crime Control in Contemporary Society', *British Journal of Criminology*, 64 (4): 445–71.

Gay, J. (1727 (1983)) *The Beggars Opera*, in J. Fuller (ed.) *Dramatic Works* Vol. 2. Oxford: Clarendon Press.

Gilroy, P. (1987) *There Ain't No Black in the Union Jack: The Cultural Politics of Race in the Nation*. London: Hutchinson.

Hall, S. (1980) *Drifting into a Law and Order Society*. London: Cobden Trust.

Hall, S., Critcher, C., Jefferson, T., Clarke, J. and Roberts, B. (1978) *Policing the Crisis: Mugging, The State and Law and Order*. London: Macmillan.

Hall, S. and Jefferson, T. (eds) (1976) *Resistance Through Rituals*. London: Hutchinson.

Hallsworth. S. and Maguire, M. (2004) *Profiling the City of London Exercise of Stop and Search*. Report for the City of London Police.

Hallsworth. S. and Richie, H. (2002) *Young People and Crime in Lambeth*. Report for Lambeth Community Safety Partnership.

Hallsworth, S. and Maguire, M. (2002) *Lambeth Community Safety Survey*. Report for Lambeth Community Safety Partnership.

Hancock, L. (2003) 'Urban regeneration and crime reduction: contradictions and dilemmas', in R. Mathews and J. Young, *The New Politics of Crime and Punishment*. Cullompton: Willan Publishing.

Harrington, V. and Mayhew, P. (2001) 'Mobile Phone Theft', *Home Office Research Study* 235. London: Home Office.

Harris, M. (ed) (1971) *1811 Dictionary of the Vulgar Toungue*. Illinois: Digest Books.

Hebdige, D. (1979) *Subculture: The Meaning of Style*. London: Methuen.

Herrenstein, R. and Murray, C. (1994) *The Bell Curve: Intelligence and Class Structure in American Life*. New York and London: Free Press.

Hobbs, D. (1988) *Doing the Business: Entrepreneurship, Detectives and the Working Class in the East End of London*. Oxford: Clarendon Press.

Hobbs, D. (2002) *Bouncers: The Art and Economics of Intimidation*. Durham: University of Durham.

Hobsbawn, E. (2000) *Bandits*. London: Weidenfeld & Nicolson.

Home Office (2003) *Prison Statistics, England and Wales, 2001*. London: HMSO.

Horkhiemer, T. and Adorno, T. (1973) *Dialectic of Enlightenment*. London: Allen Lane.

Hughes, G. and Edwards, A. (eds) (2002) *The Local Politics of Crime Control*. Cullompton: Willan Publishing.

Isabel, S.T.A. (ed.) (1953) *Anglo-Norman Political Songs*. Oxford: Blackwell.

Jameson, F. (1984) 'Postmodernism or the Cultural Logic of Late Capitalism', *New Left Review*, 146: 53–92.

Jenson, A. (1969) 'How Much Can we Boost IQ and Scholastic Achievement?', *Harvard Educational Review*, 39: 1–123.

Johnson, C.C. (1734) *A General History of the Lives and Adventures of the Most Famous Highwaymen*. London: Janeway.

Johnson, L. (1998) 'Street Crime in England and Wales', in I.K. McKenzie (ed.), *Law, Power and Justice in England and Wales*. Westport: Praegar Publishers.

Kaspersson, M. (2003) 'The Great Murder Mystery or Explaining Declining Homicide Rates', in C.E.B. Godfrey and G. Tunstall (eds), *Comparative Histories of Crime*. Cullompton: Willan Publishers.

Katz, J. (1988) *The Seductions of Crime: The Moral and Sensual Attractions in Doing Evil*. New York: Basic Books.

Kershaw, C. and colleagues (2001) *The 2001 British Crime Survey: First Results England and Wales*. London: Home Office.

Kershaw, C. and colleagues (2000) 'The British Crime Survey', *Home Office Crime Bulletin* 18/00. London: Home Office.

King, P. (1987) 'Newspaper reporting, prosecution practice and perceptions of urban crime: the Colchester crime wave of 1765', *Continuity and Change*, 2: 423–54.

Klein, N. (2001) *No Logo*. New York: Flamingo.

Linebough, P. (1991) *The London Hanged: Crime and Civil Society in the 18th Century*. London: Allen Lane.

Mayhew, H. (1985) *London Labour and the London Poor, Vol 1*. London: Penguin Books.
Mayhew, H. (1985) *London Labour and the London Poor, Vol 4, Those Who Will Not Work*. London: Penguin Books.
Merton, R. (1953) *Social Theory and Social Structure*. New York: Free Press.
Miles, S. (2000) *Youth Life Styles in a Changing World*. Milton Keynes: Open University Press.
Miles, W.A. (ed.) (1839) *Poverty, Mendacity and Crime*. London.
Morrison, A. (1894) *A Child of the Jago*. London.
Murray, C. (1990) *The Emerging British Underclass*. London: Institute for Economic Affairs.

Noyes, A. (1928) *Ballads and Poems*. S.I. Blackwood.

Oftel (2002) Key trends in fixed and mobile telephony, and Internet – residential consumers – 17 June 2002.
http://www.oftel.gov.uk/publications/research/2002/trenr0602
Oftel (2003) Trends in Mobile Phone Use.
http://www.oftel.gov.uk/publications/research/2003/q12mobr0403.htm#chapterthree

Pearson, G. (1983) *Hooligan: a History of Respectable Fears*. London: Routledge.
Phillips, M. (2002) Britain's Deadly Drug Policy. *Daily Mail*.
Phillips, M. (2003) Gun Law Comes to England. *Daily Mail*.
Platt, A. (1978) 'Street Crime: A View From the Left', *Crime and Social Justice*, 9.
Pope, W. (1670) *The Memoires of Monsieur Du Vall*. London: Cambridge University Library.
Porter, P. (1994) *London: A Social History*. London: Penguin Books.

Rawlings, P. (1999) *Crime and Power: A History of Criminal Justice, 1688–1998*. London and New York: Longman.
Rawson, J. (ed.) (1889) *Henry of Knighton's Chronicle*. London: HMSO.
Reiner, R. (1997) 'Media Made Criminality', in R.M.M. Maguire and R. Reiner (eds), *Oxford Handbook of Criminology*. Oxford: Oxford University Press.
Rutherford, J. (1997) Introduction. *Soundings*. Summer, 6: 112–26.

Scarman, L. (1981) *The Brixton Disorders 10–12 April 1981: Report by the Rt. Honourable the Lord Scarman*. London: HMSO.
Seabrook, J. (1978) *What Went Wrong? Working People and the Ideals of the Labour Movement*. London: Victor Gollancz.
Shore, H. (1999) *Artful Dodgers*. Woodbridge: Boydell Press.

Shore, H. (1999) 'Cross coves, buzzers and general sorts of prigs: juvenile crime and the criminal "underworld" in the early nineteenth century', *The British Journal of Criminology*, 39: 10–24.

Shore, H. (2003) 'Inventing the juvenile delinquent in Europe', in C.E.B. Godfrey and G. Dunstall (eds), *Comparative Histories of Crime*. Cullompton: Willan Publishing.

Smith, H.O.J. (2003) 'The Nature of Personal Robbery', *Home Office Research Study 254*. London: Home Office.

Spierenburg, P. (1998) *The Spectacle of Suffering*. Cambridge: Cambridge University Press.

Spraggs, G. (2001) *Outlaws and Highwaymen: The Cult of the Robber in England from the Middle Ages to the Nineteenth Century*. London: Pimlico.

Sutherland, E. and Cressey, D. (1979) *Principles of Criminology*. Chicago: Lippincott.

Sutton, M. (1998) *Handling Stolen Goods and Theft: A Market Reduction Approach*, Home Office Research and Statistics Directorate, Research Findings No. 69, London: HMSO.

Sykes G. and Matza, D. (1957) 'Techniques of Neutralization: a Theory of Delinquency', *American Sociological Review*, 22: 664–70.

Taylor, J. (1973 (1630)) *All the Workes of John Taylor the Water Poet*. Menston, Yorkshire: Scholar Press.

Tonry, M. (2004) *Punishment and Politics: Evidence and Emulation in the Making of British Crime Control Policy*. Cullompton: Willan Publishing.

Wartella, B. (1995) 'Media and Problem Behaviours in Young People', in D.S.M. Rutter (ed.), *Psychological Disorders in Young People*. London: Wiley.

Willis, P. (1977) *Learning to Labour*. Farnborough: Saxon House.

Winslow, G. (2003) 'Capital Crimes: The Corporate Economy of Violence', in P. Wright (ed.), *Prison Nation: The Warehousing of America's Poor*. New York and London: Routledge.

Wollstonecraft, M. (ed.) (1989 (1794)) *An Historical and Moral View of the French Revolution in Works*. London: William Pickering.

Young, J. (1979) 'Left Idealism, Reformism and Beyond', in R.K.B. Fine, J. Lea, S. Picciotto and J. Young (eds), *Capitalism and the Rule of Law*. London: Hutchinson.

Young, J. (1986) 'The Tasks for a Realist Criminology', *Contemporary Crisis*, 2: 337–56.

Young, J. (1997) 'Left Realist Criminology: Radical in its Analysis, Realist in its Policy', in M.M. Maguire and R. Reiner (eds), *The Oxford Handbook of Criminology*. Oxford: Clarendon Press.

Young, J. (2001) *The Exclusive Society: Social Exclusion, Crime and Difference in Late Modernity*. London: Sage.

Young, J. and Lea, J. (1984) *What is to be Done about Law and Order?* London: Penguin.

Index